EASY PIANO

the twilight saga
new moon

MUSIC FROM THE MOTION PICTURE SOUNDTRACK

SUMMIT ENTERTAINMENT PRESENTS "THE TWILIGHT SAGA: NEW MOON"
A TEMPLE HILL PRODUCTION IN ASSOCIATION WITH MAVERICK / IMPRINT AND SUNSWEPT ENTERTAINMENT KRISTEN STEWART ROBERT PATTINSON TAYLOR LAUTNER ASHLEY GREENE RACHELLE LEFEVRE BILLY BURKE PETER FACINELLI ELIZABETH REASER NIKKI REED KELLAN LUTZ JACKSON RATHBONE ANNA KENDRICK WITH MICHAEL SHEEN AND DAKOTA FANNING CASTING BY JOSEPH MIDDLETON, C.S.A. MUSIC BY ALEXANDRE DESPLAT MUSIC SUPERVISOR ALEXANDRA PATSAVAS COSTUME DESIGNER TISH MONAGHAN EDITOR PETER LAMBERT PRODUCTION DESIGNER DAVID BRISBIN DIRECTOR OF PHOTOGRAPHY JAVIER AGUIRRESAROBE CO-PRODUCER BILL BANNERMAN EXECUTIVE PRODUCERS MARTY BOWEN GREG MOORADIAN MARK MORGAN GUY OSEARY PRODUCED BY WYCK GODFREY KAREN ROSENFELT BASED ON THE NOVEL "NEW MOON" BY STEPHENIE MEYER

PG-13 PARENTS STRONGLY CAUTIONED
Some Material May Be Inappropriate for Children Under 13
Some Violence and Action

11.20.09
www.newmoonthemovie.com

ISBN 978-1-4234-9011-1

HAL•LEONARD®
CORPORATION
7777 W. BLUEMOUND RD. P.O. BOX 13819 MILWAUKEE, WI 53213

Visit Hal Leonard Online at
www.halleonard.com

MEET ME ON THE EQUINOX

Words and Music by BENJAMIN GIBBARD,
CHRISTOPHER WALLA, NICHOLAS HARMER
and JASON McGERR

Moderate Rock

With pedal

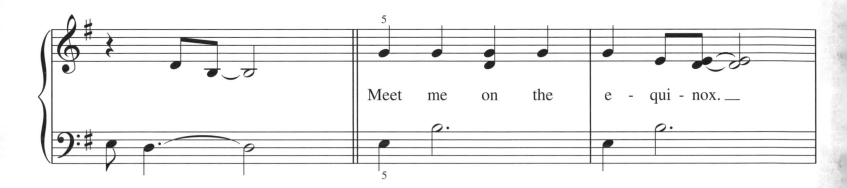

Meet me on the e - qui - nox. __

Meet me half - way. The sun is perched at its

G/D

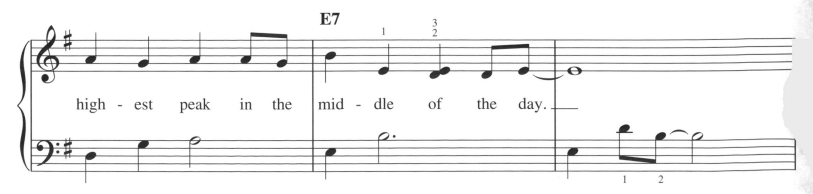

high - est peak in the mid - dle of the day. __

E7

Let me give my love to you, ___ let me take your

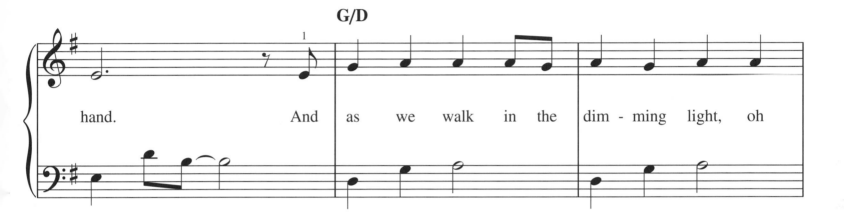

G/D

hand. And as we walk in the dim - ming light, oh

E7   **To Coda** ⊕ **C**

dar - ling, un - der - stand ___ that ev - 'ry - thing,

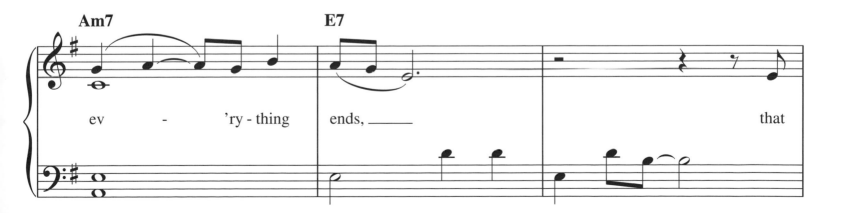

Am7   **E7**

ev - 'ry - thing ends, ___ that

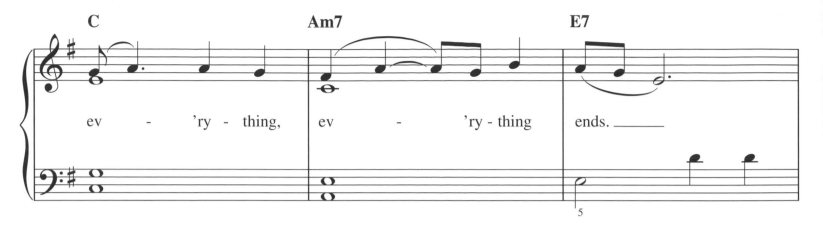

ev - 'ry - thing, ev - 'ry - thing ends. ____

Meet me on your best be - hav - ior, meet me at your

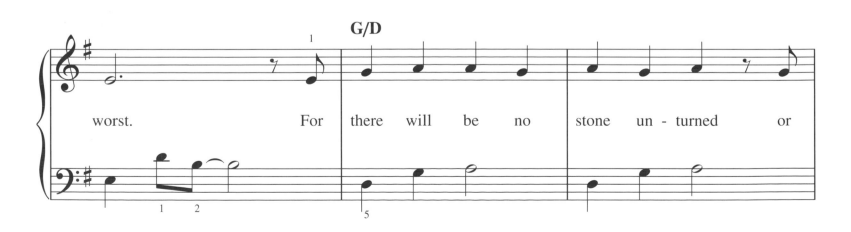

worst. For there will be no stone un - turned or

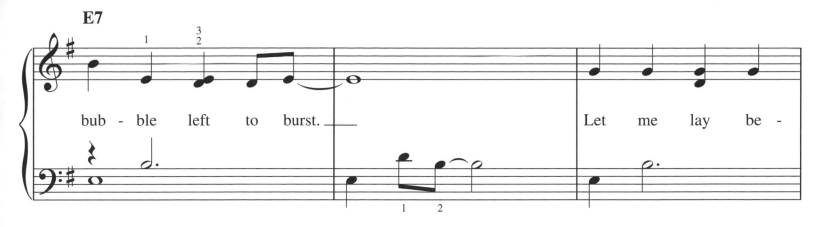

bub - ble left to burst. ___ Let me lay be -

side you, dar - ling, let me be your man and

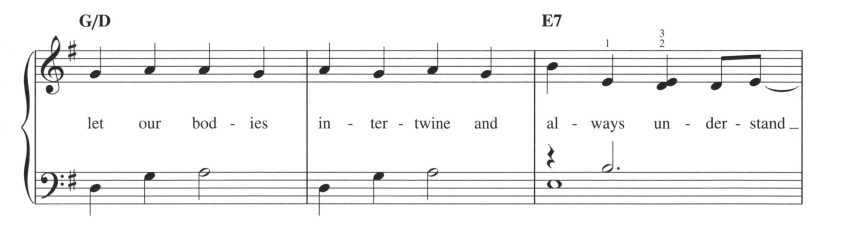

let our bod - ies in - ter - twine and al - ways un - der - stand ___

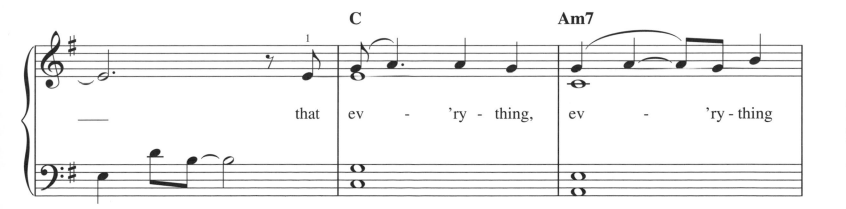

___ that ev - 'ry - thing, ev - 'ry - thing

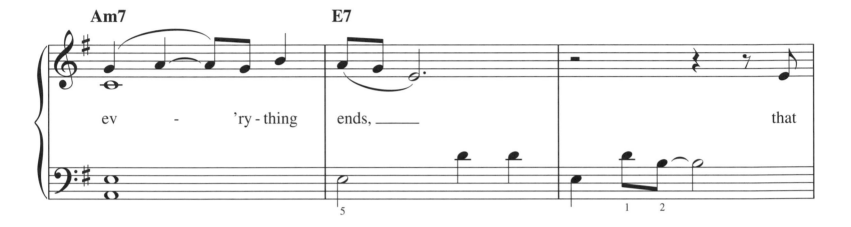

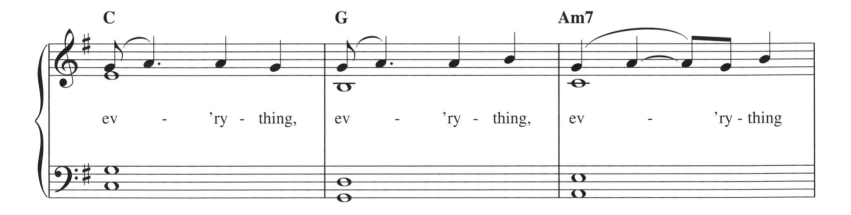

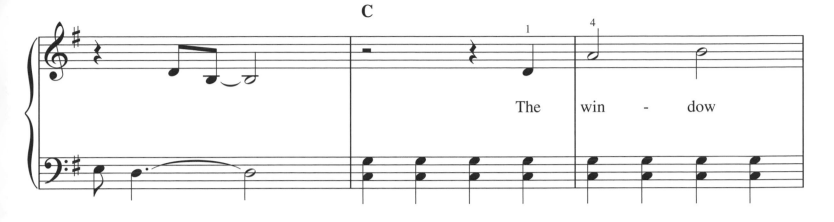

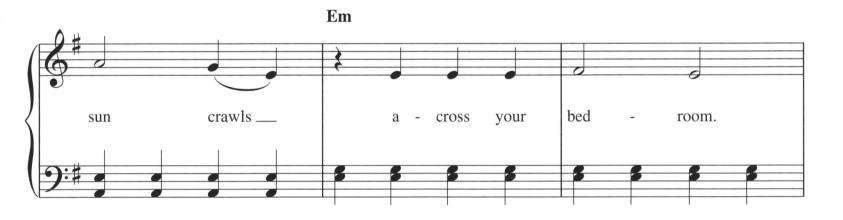

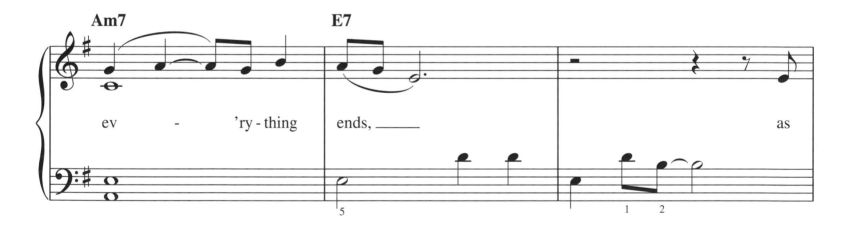

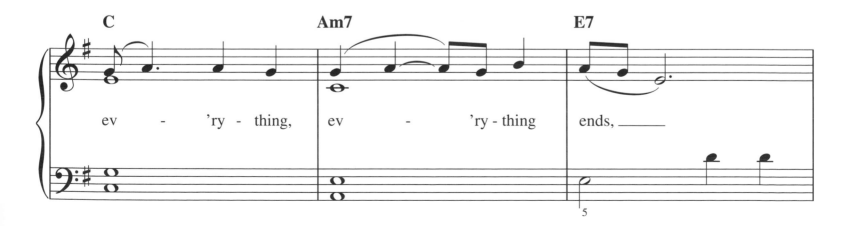

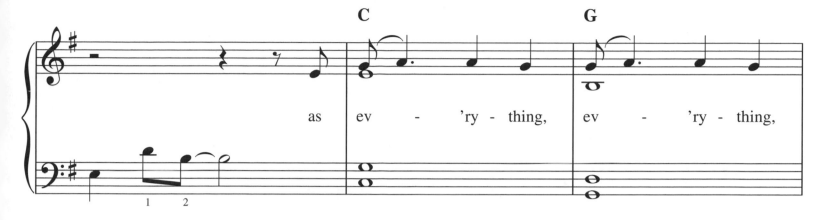

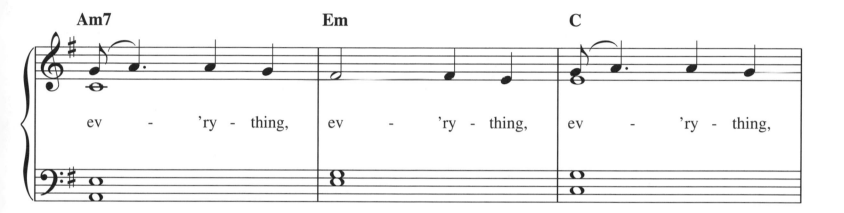

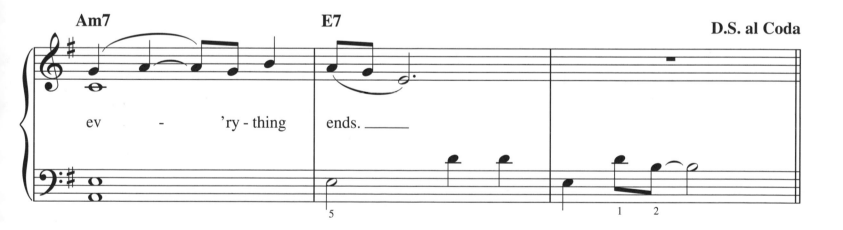

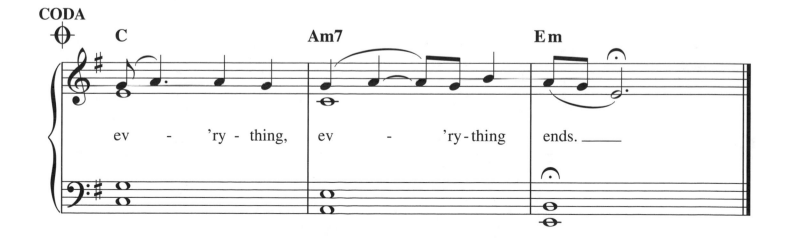

FRIENDS

Words and Music by RUSSELL MARSDEN,
EMMA RICHARDSON and MATTHEW HAYWARD

Moderate moody Rock

All my life I've been search-in' for some-thin', some-thin' I can put my fin-ger on.

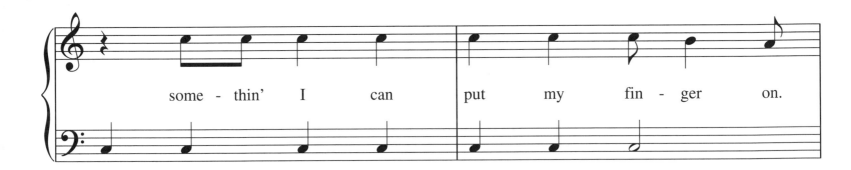

Maybe I've been livin' for the week-end. Maybe I've been livin' for the si-ren song.

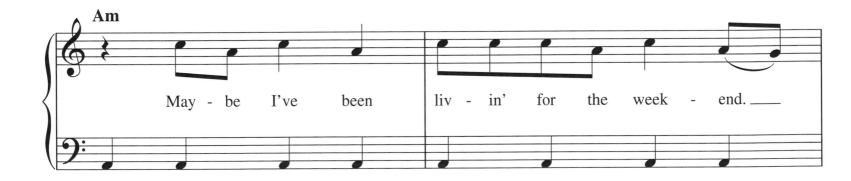

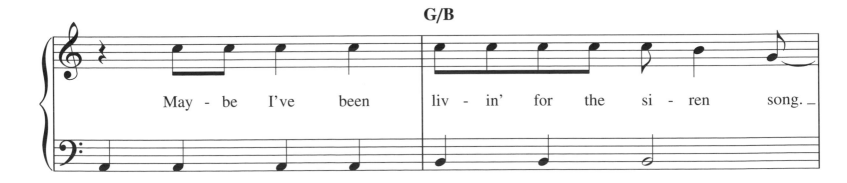

But ev'ry Fri - day, just a - bout mid - night, __ all my prob - lems

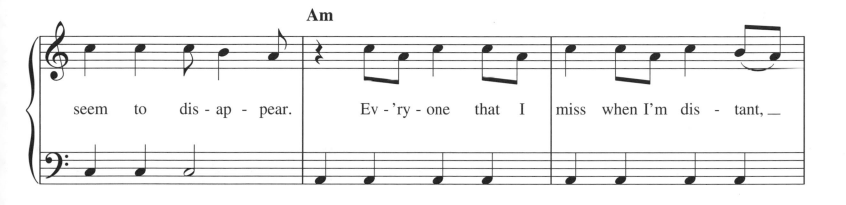

seem to dis - ap - pear. Ev - 'ry - one that I miss when I'm dis - tant, __

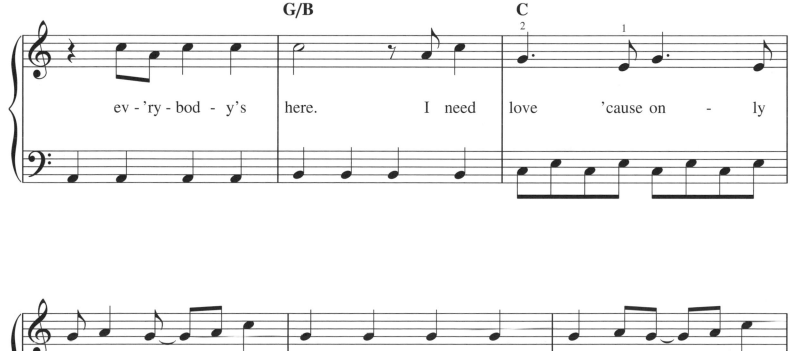

ev - 'ry - bod - y's here. I need love 'cause on - ly

love is true. __ I need ev - 'ry wak - in' hour with you __ and my

friends   'cause they're   so   beau-ti - ful. __ Yeah, my   friends   they are   so

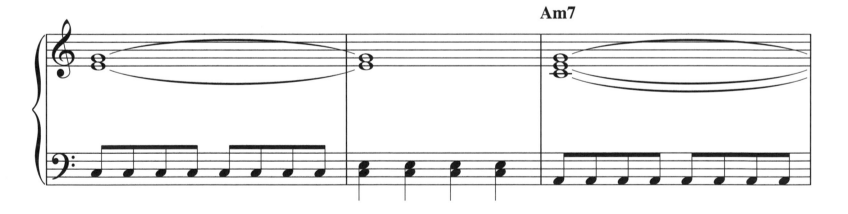

beau-ti - ful. __ They're my   friends.

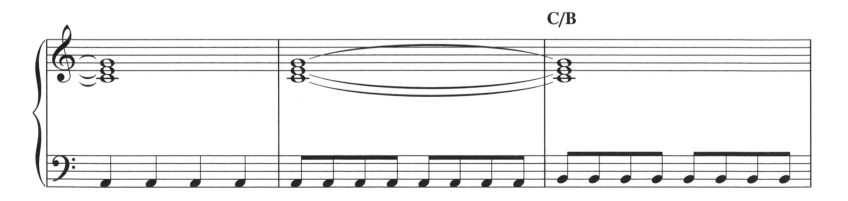

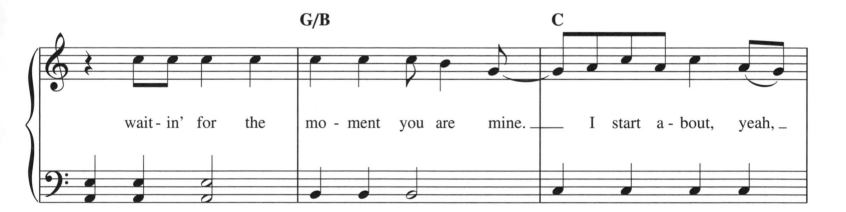

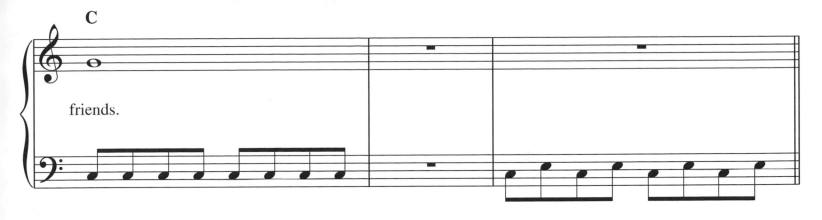

friends.

They're my friends. They're my

friends. They're my friends.

They're my friends. friends.

HEARING DAMAGE

Words and Music by
THOM YORKE

Moderate Techno groove

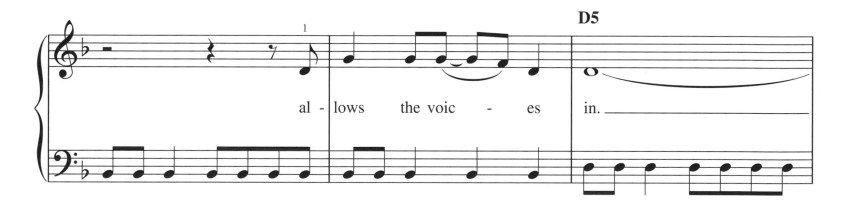

Bb5

push you off the path, _____

D5

with their low fre-quen-cy whin - ing. _____

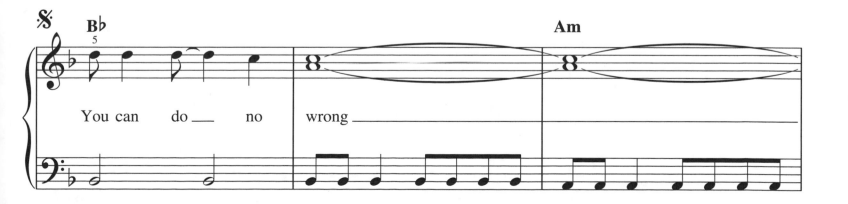

Bb

Am

You can do ___ no wrong _____

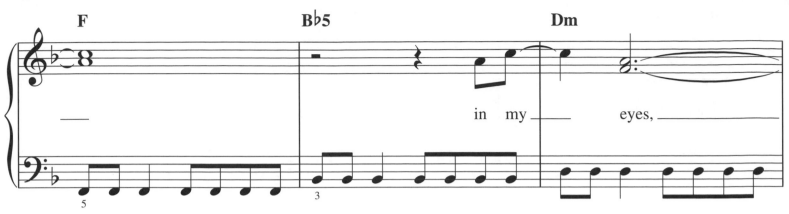

in my eyes,

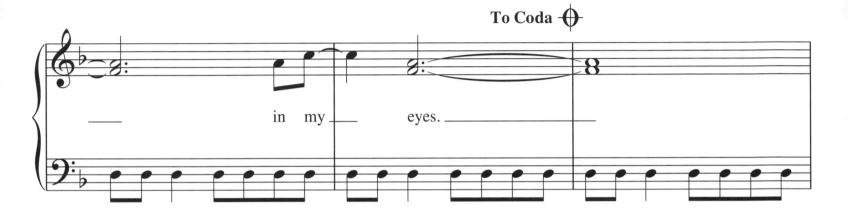

To Coda ⊕

in my eyes.

You can do no wrong

in my eyes, in my eyes.

A drunk - en sales - man, your hear - ing dam - age. Your
speak - ers are blow - ing, your ears are wreck - ing. Your

mind is rest - less. They say you're get - ting bet - ter but
hear - ing dam - age. You wish you felt____ bet - ter. You

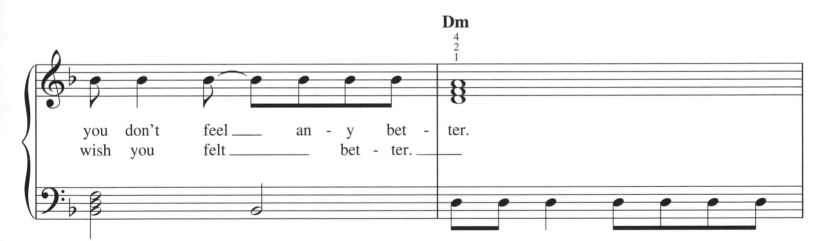

Dm

you don't feel____ an - y bet - ter.
wish you felt_____ bet - ter.____

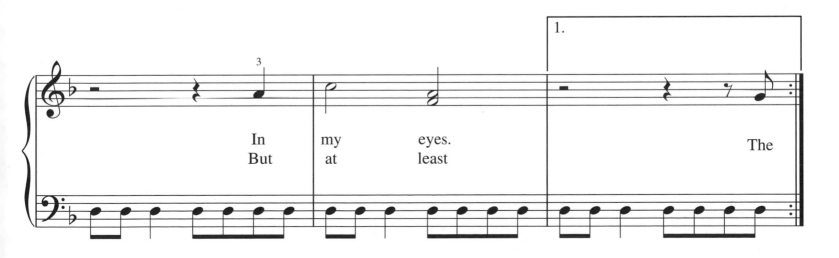

1.

In my eyes.
But at least

The

you can do __ no wrong _____

in my __

__ eyes, in my __ eyes.

D.S. al Coda

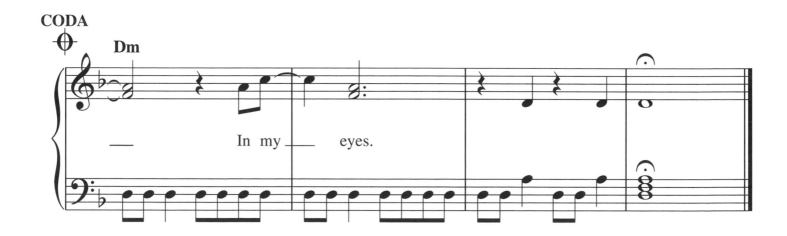

CODA

__ In my __ eyes.

POSSIBILITY

Words and Music by
LYKKE LI ZACHRISSON

Slow, moody ballad, in 2

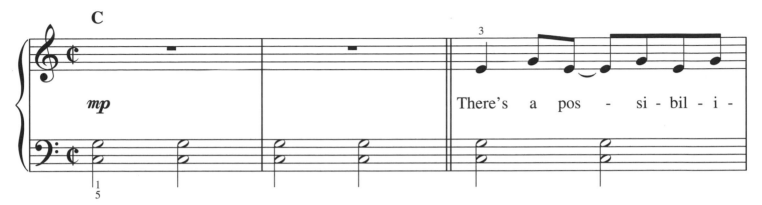

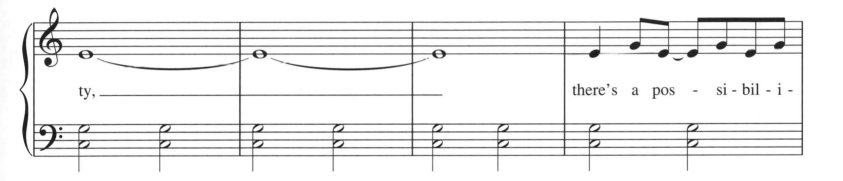

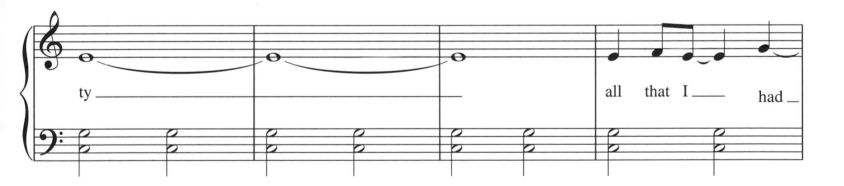

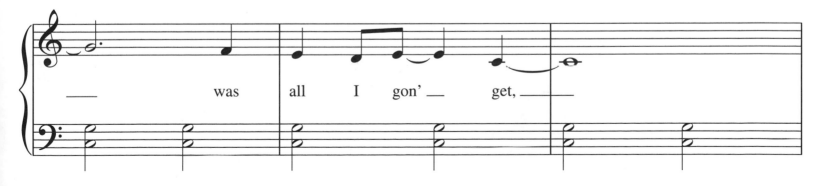

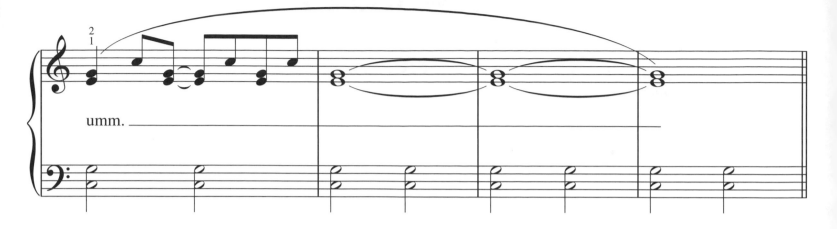

umm.

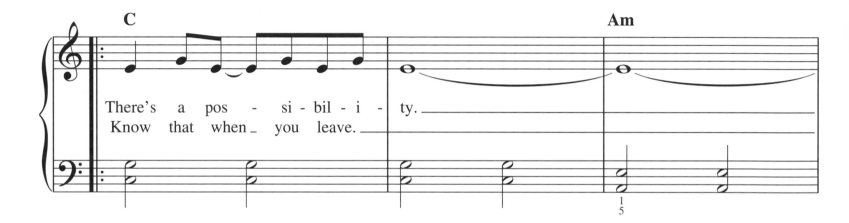

C   Am

There's a pos - si - bil - i - ty.
Know that when you leave.

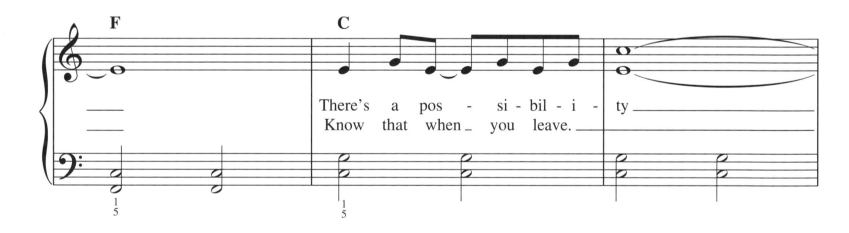

F   C

There's a pos - si - bil - i - ty
Know that when you leave.

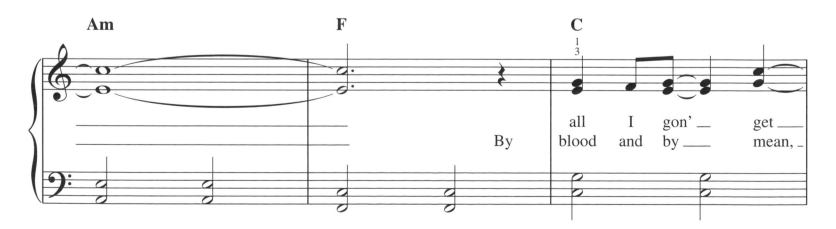

Am   F   C

           all I gon' get
By blood and by mean,

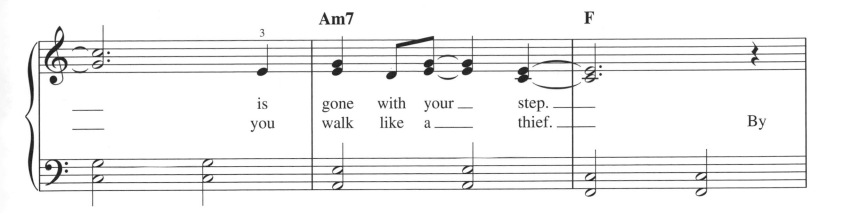

is gone with your ___ step. ___
you walk like a ___ thief. ___
By

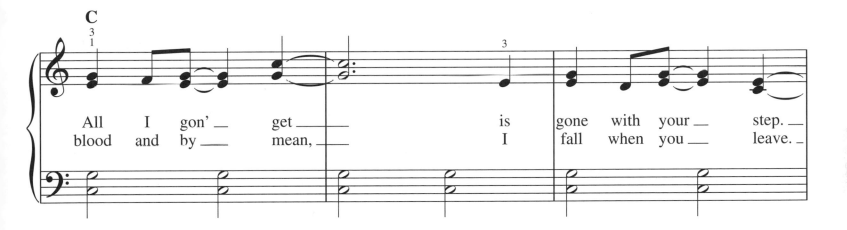

All I gon' ___ get ___ is gone with your ___ step. ___
blood and by ___ mean, ___ I fall when you ___ leave. ___

So tell me when you hear my heart ___

___ stop. You're the on - ly one who knows. ___

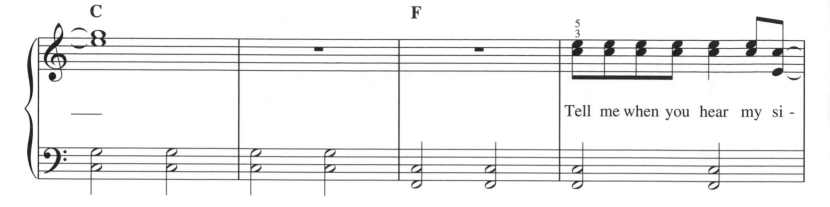

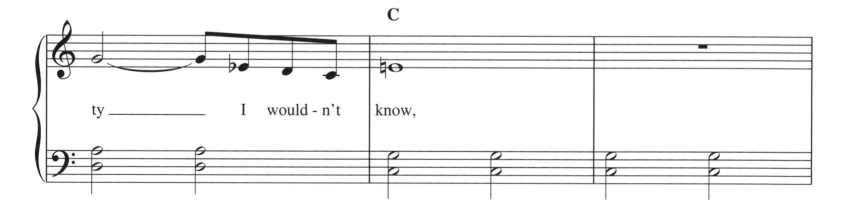

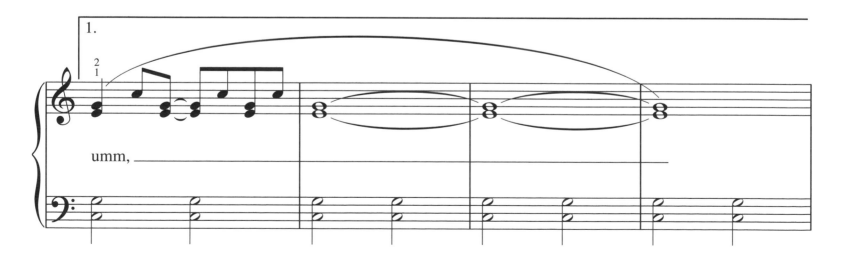

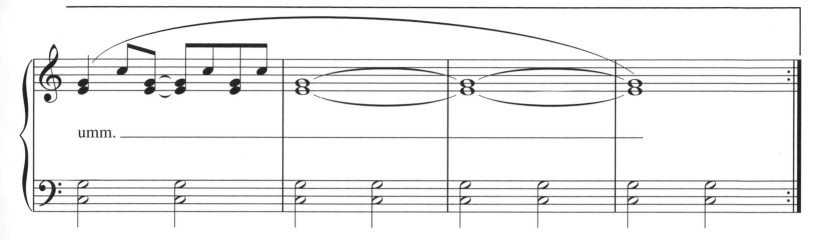

umm. _____

F   **C**

So tell me when my sigh is o - ver. _____

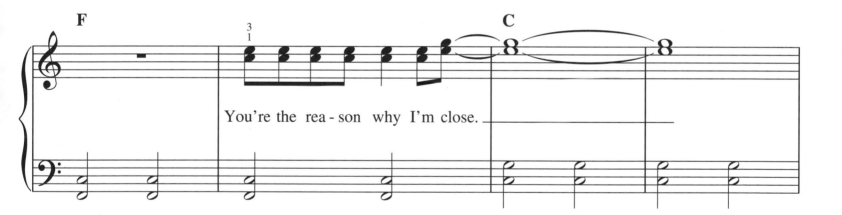

F   **C**

You're the rea - son why I'm close. _____

F   **C**

Tell me when you hear me fall - in'. _____ There's a

pos - si - bil - i - ty _____ it would-n't show,

umm, _____

umm. _____

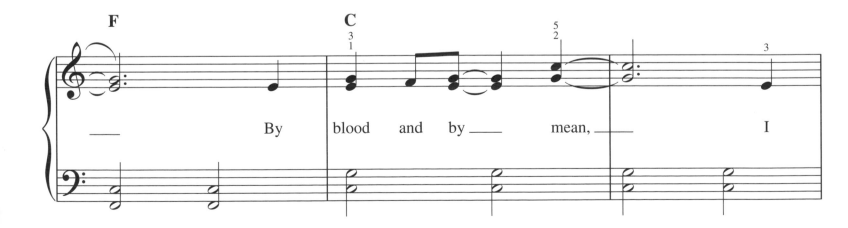

By blood and by ___ mean, ___ I

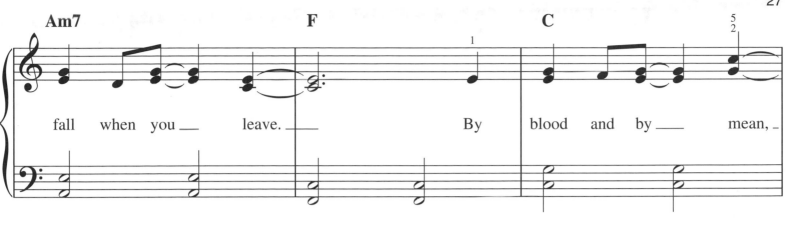

fall when you leave. By blood and by mean,

I'll fol - low your lead,

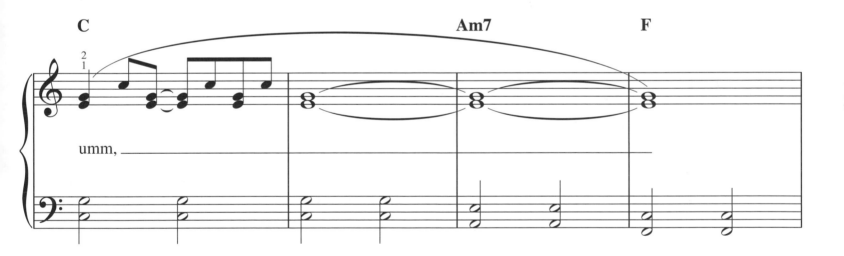

umm,

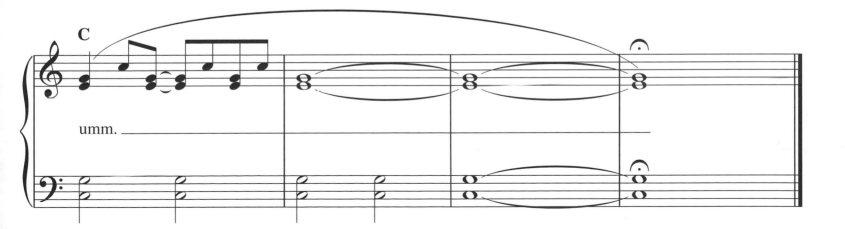

umm.

A WHITE DEMON LOVE SONG

Words and Music by
THE KILLERS

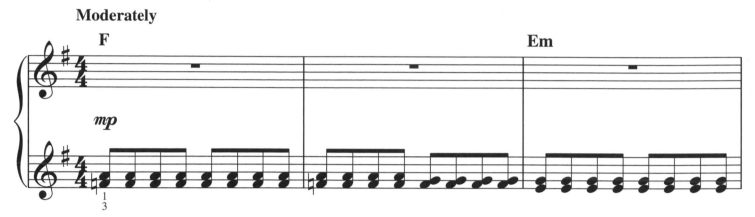

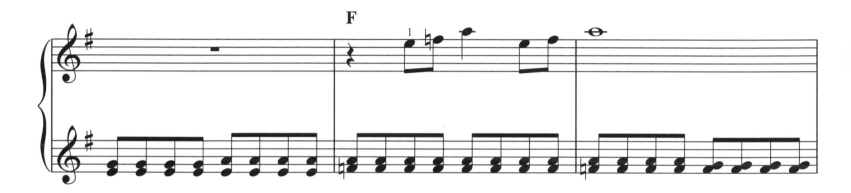

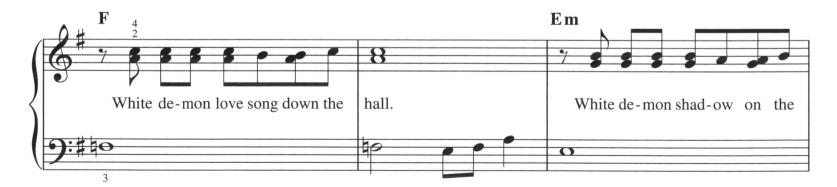

White de-mon love song down the hall. White de-mon shad-ow on the

road. Back up your mind, there is a call.

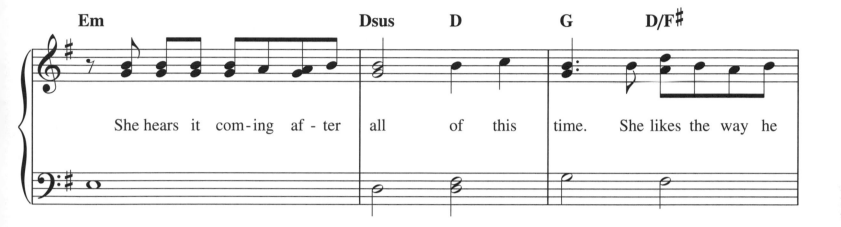

She hears it com-ing af-ter all of this time. She likes the way he

sings white de-mon love songs in her dreams. ____

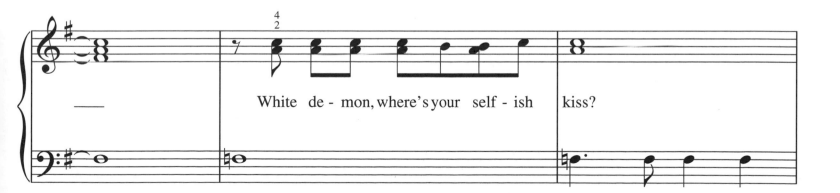

____ White de-mon, where's your self-ish kiss?

White de-mon sor-row will ar - range.

Let's not for-get a - bout the

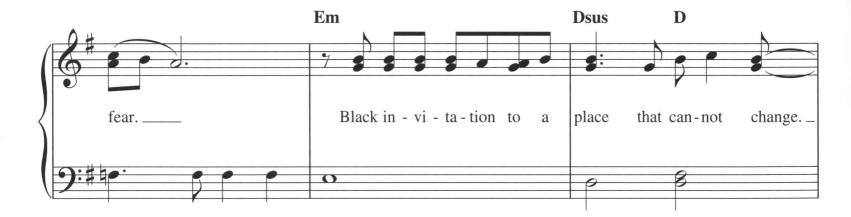

fear. _____

Black in - vi - ta - tion to a place that can-not change. _

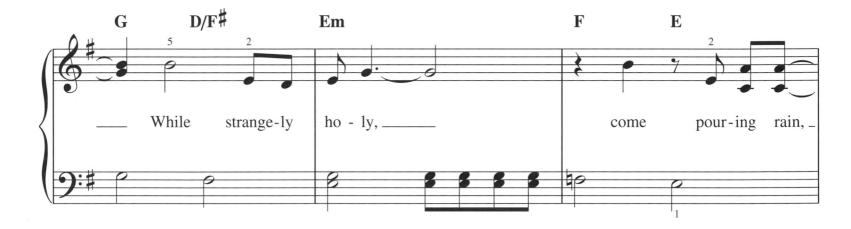

_ While strange-ly ho - ly, _____

come pour-ing rain, _

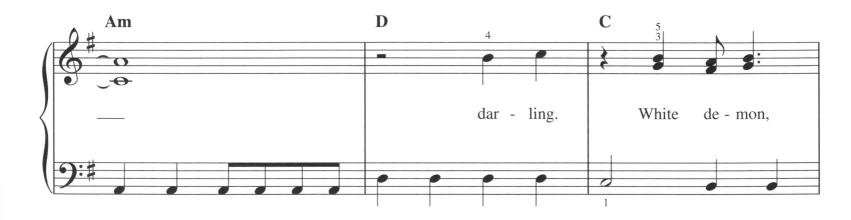

_ dar - ling.

White de - mon,

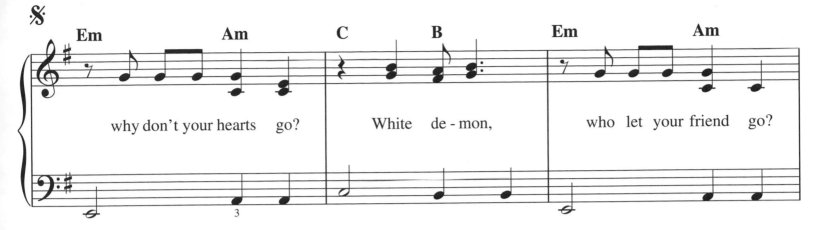

why don't your hearts go? White de - mon, who let your friend go?

White de - mon, why don't your hearts go? White de - mon,

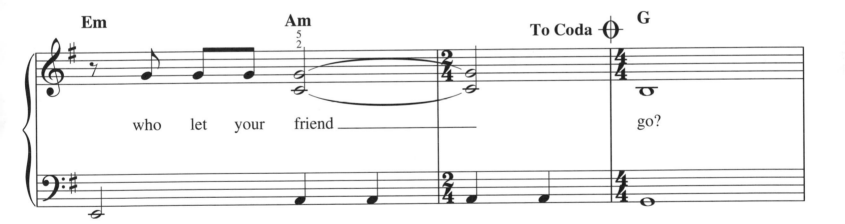

who let your friend _____ go?

Let us be in love. _____ (Let us be in love.) _____

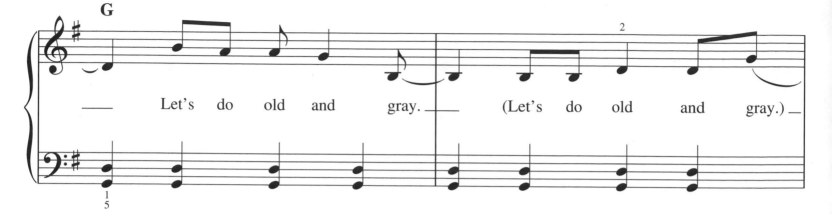

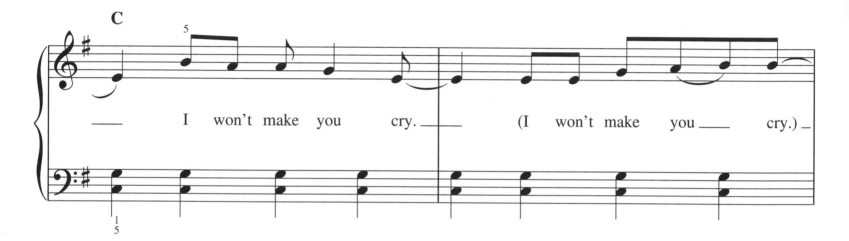

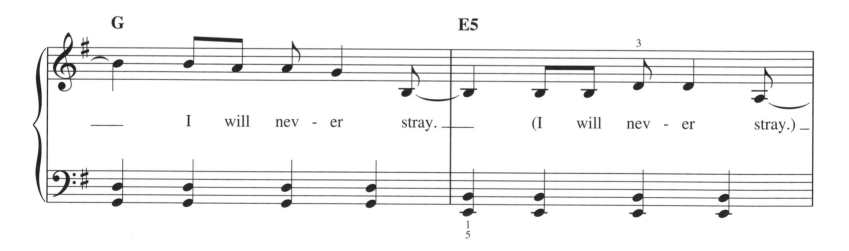

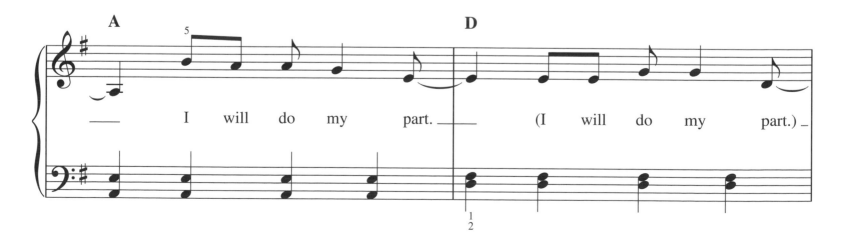

D.S. al Coda

Let us be in love _____ to - night. White de - mon,

CODA

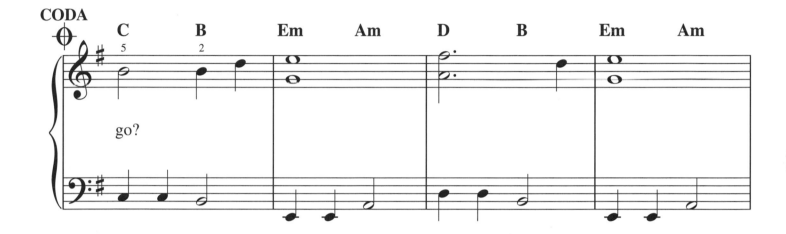

go?

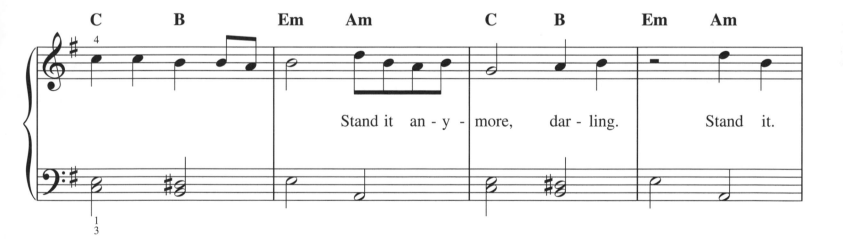

Stand it an - y - more, dar - ling. Stand it.

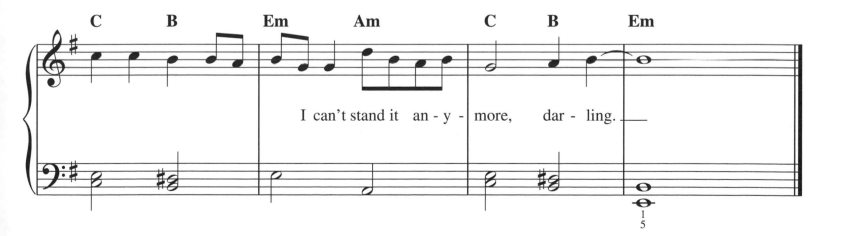

I can't stand it an - y - more, dar - ling. _____

SATELLITE HEART

Words and Music by
ANYA MARINA

Moderately

So pret - ty, _____ so

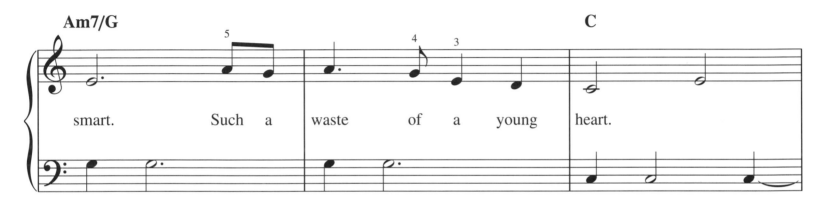

smart. Such a waste of a young heart.

What a pi - ty. _____ What a

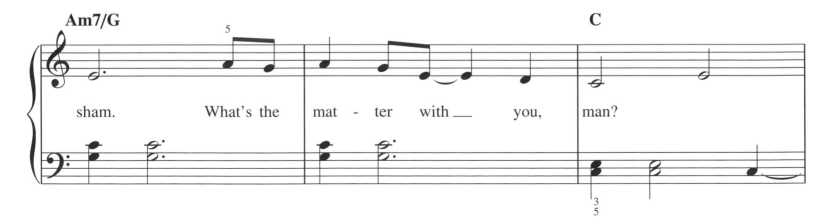

sham. What's the mat - ter with _ you, man?

Don't you see it's | wrong? Can't you get it
Call on all your | girls, don't for - get the

right? Out of | mind and out - ta | sight.
boys. Put a | lid on all that | noise.

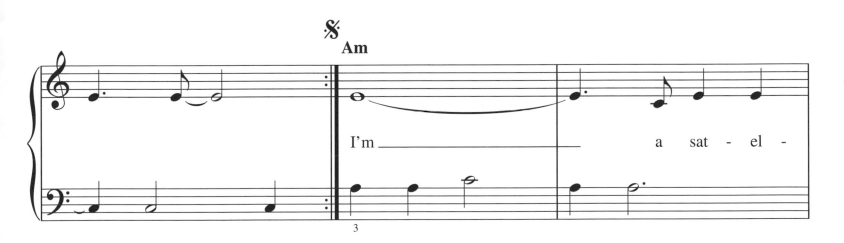

I'm _____ | a sat - el -

lite heart | lost in ___ | the dark. __

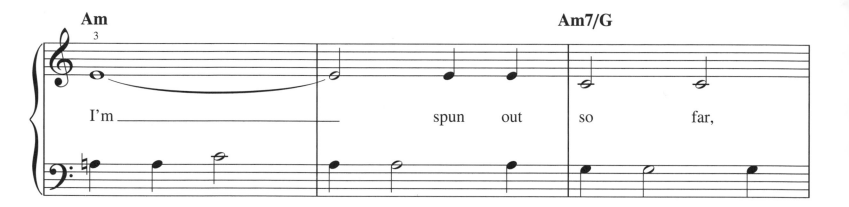

I'm _____ spun out so far,

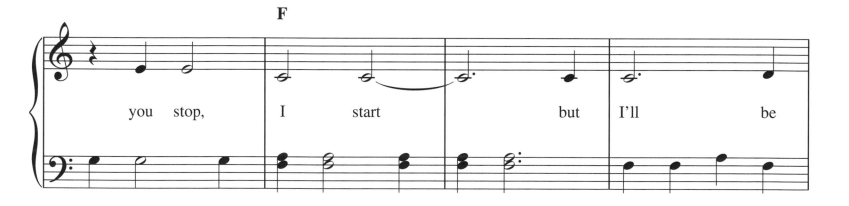

you stop, I start but I'll be

To Coda ⊕

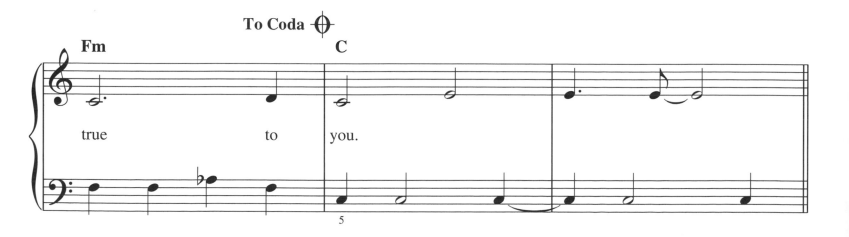

true to you.

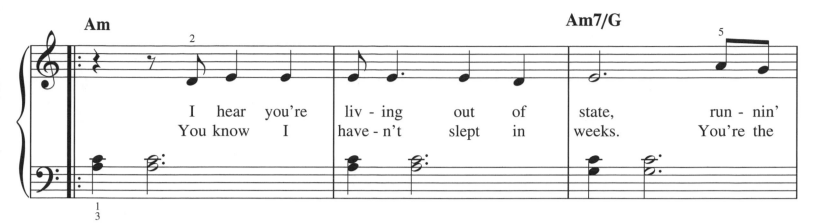

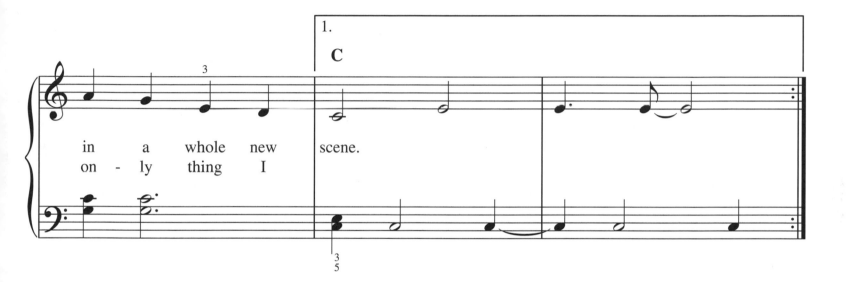

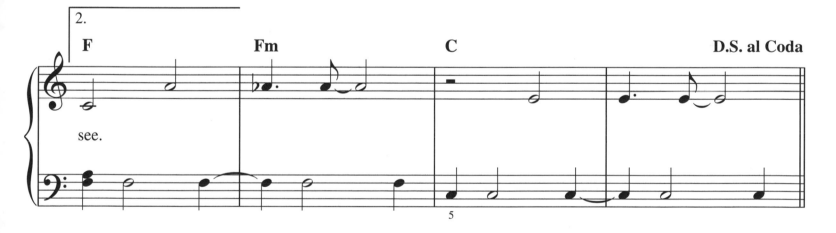

what you do,
yeah,

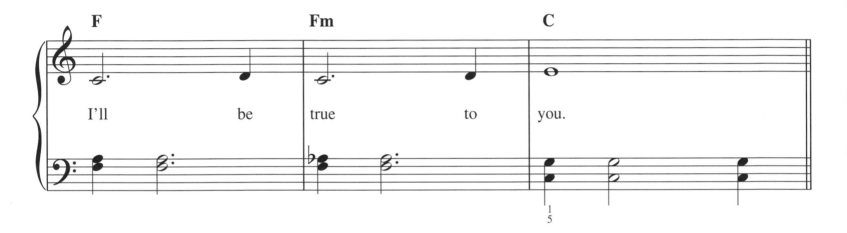

I'll be true to you.

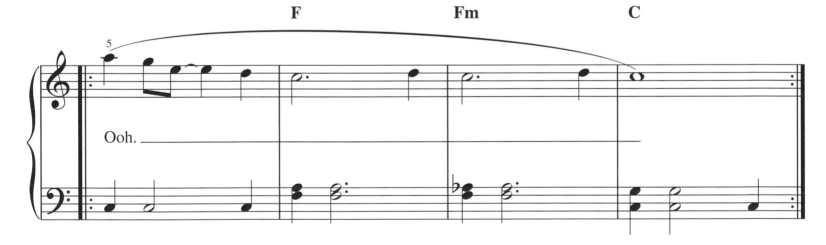

Ooh. _____

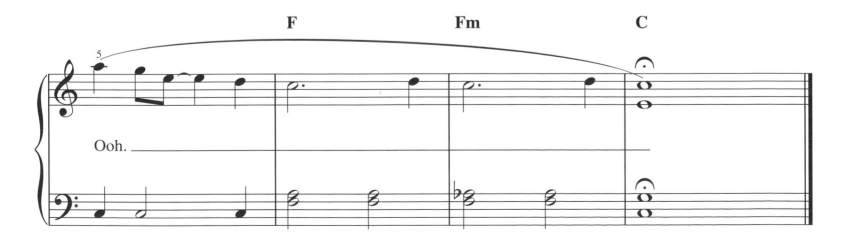

Ooh. _____

I BELONG TO YOU
(New Moon Remix)

Words and Music by
MATTHEW BELLAMY

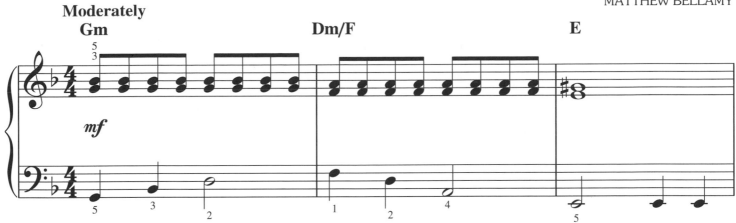

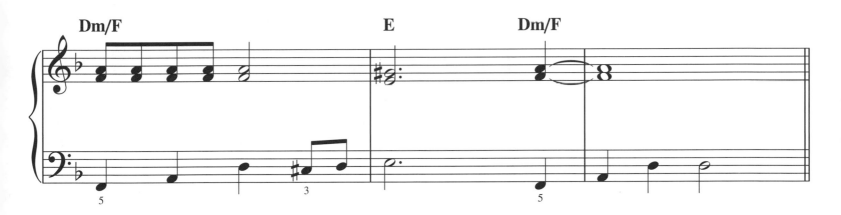

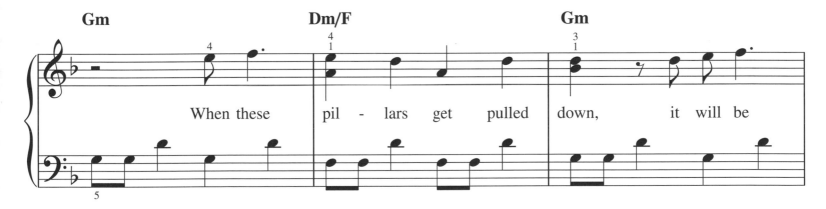

When these pil - lars get pulled down, it will be

you who wears the crown, and I'll owe ev - 'ry - thing to

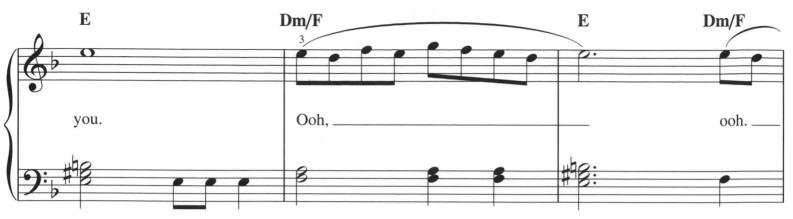

you.　　　　Ooh, _____　　ooh. ____

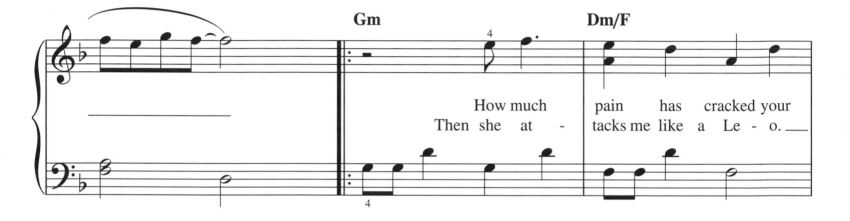

_____

How much　　pain　has　cracked your
Then she at - tacks me like a　Le - o. ___

soul?

soul?　　　How　much　　love　would　make　you
____　when　my　heart　is　split　like　Ri - o, _____

whole?　　　You're my　　guid - ing　light - ning
____　Well, I as - sure　you　my　debts　are

E   Am   F

strike.
real.   I can't find the words to
        I can't find the words to

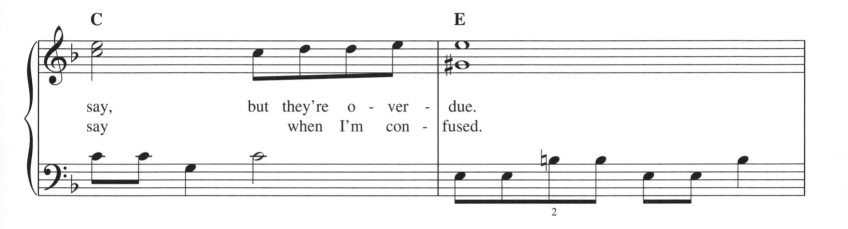

C   E

say,   but they're o - ver - due.
say   when I'm con - fused.

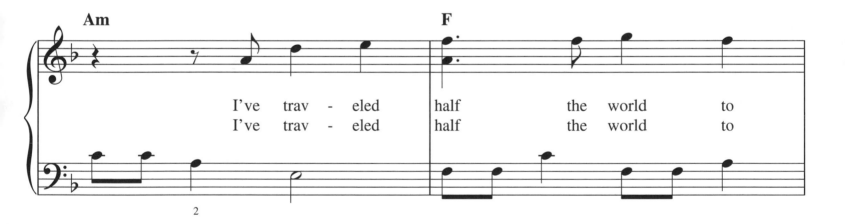

Am   F

I've trav - eled half the world to
I've trav - eled half the world to

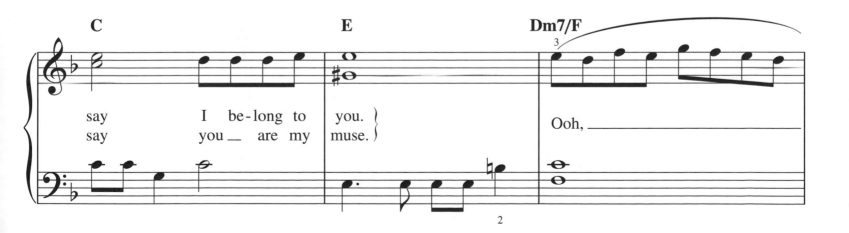

C   E   Dm7/F

say I be-long to you.
say you __ are my muse.   Ooh, _____

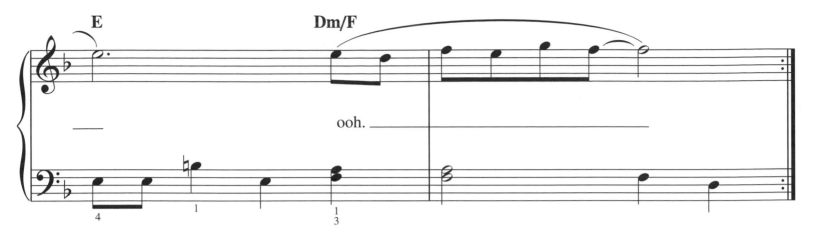

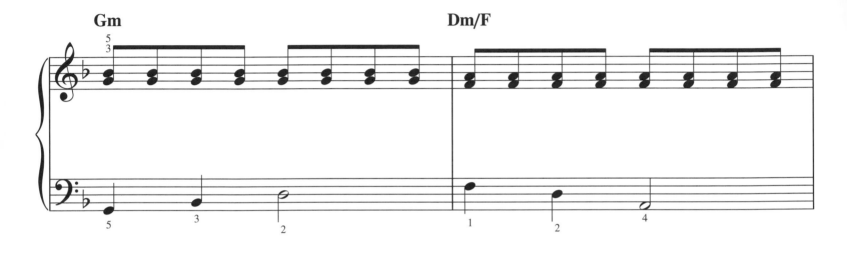

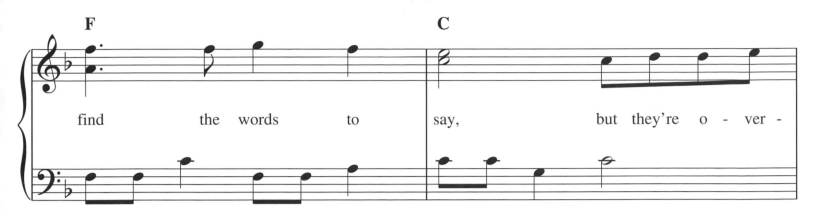

find the words to say, but they're o - ver -

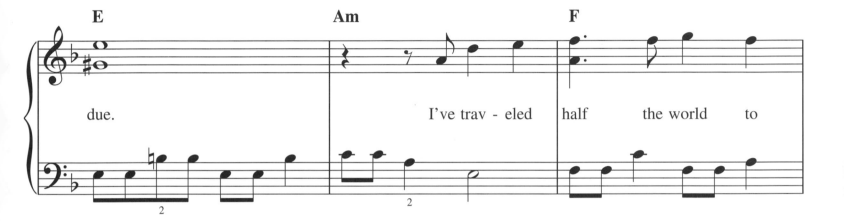

due. I've trav - eled half the world to

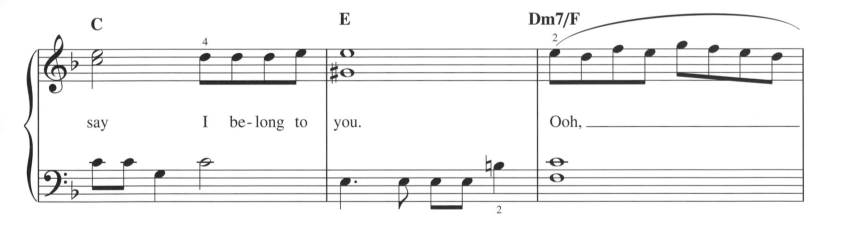

say I be - long to you. Ooh, ____

____ ooh. ____

ROSLYN

Words and Music by
JUSTIN VERNON

Moderately slow, in 1

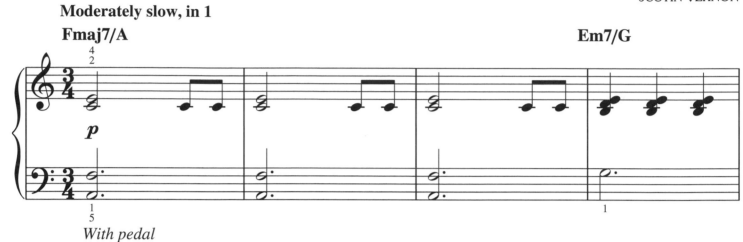

With pedal

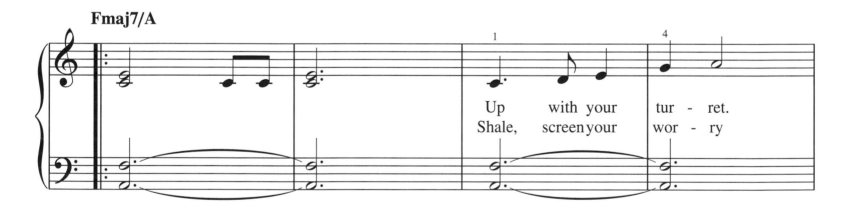

Up   with your   tur - ret.
Shale,   screen your   wor - ry

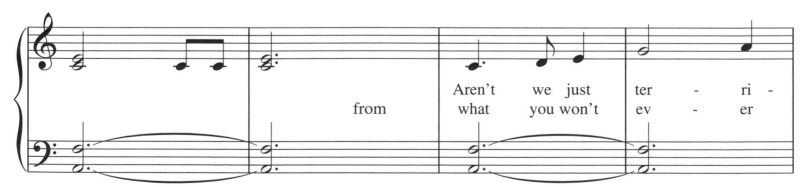

from
Aren't   we just   ter - ri -
what   you won't   ev - er

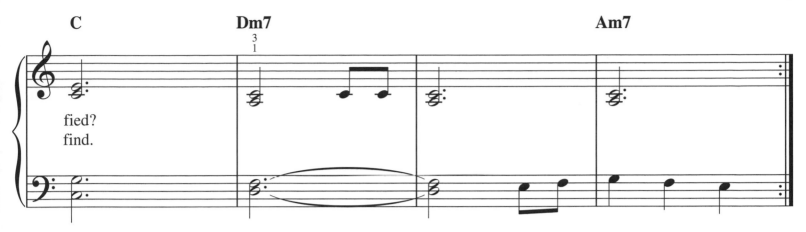

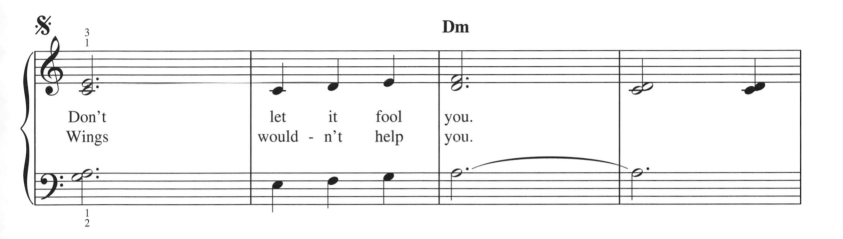

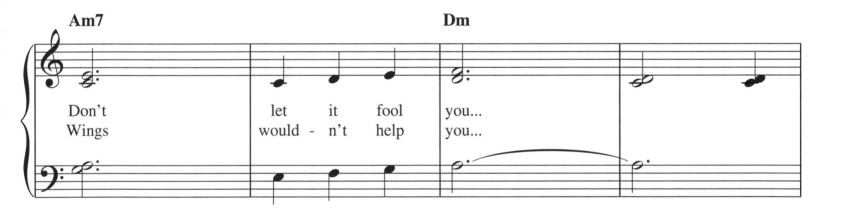

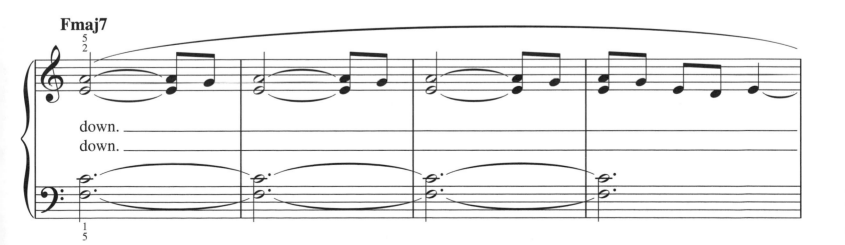

Down's _____ sit - ting
Down _____ fills the

C   **F/A**

round,   folds   in the
ground,   grav - i - ty's

G   **To Coda** ⊕

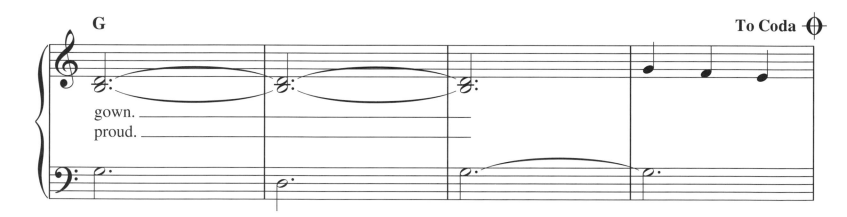

gown. _____
proud. _____

Am

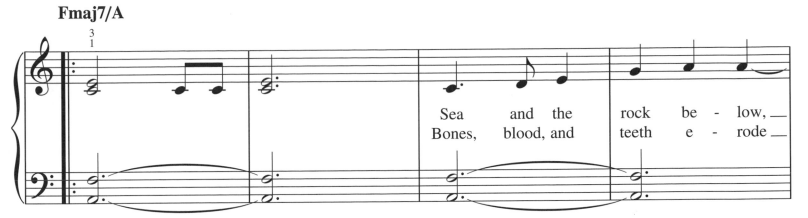

Fmaj7/A

Sea and the rock be - low, ___
Bones, blood, and teeth e - rode ___

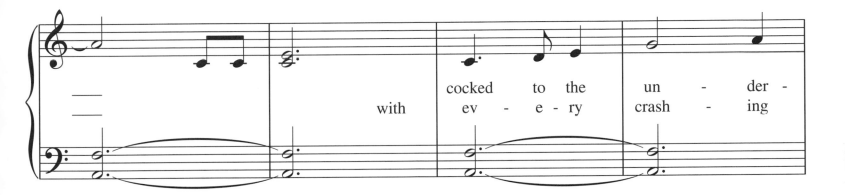

___ with cocked to the un - der - ing
___ ev - e - ry crash - ing

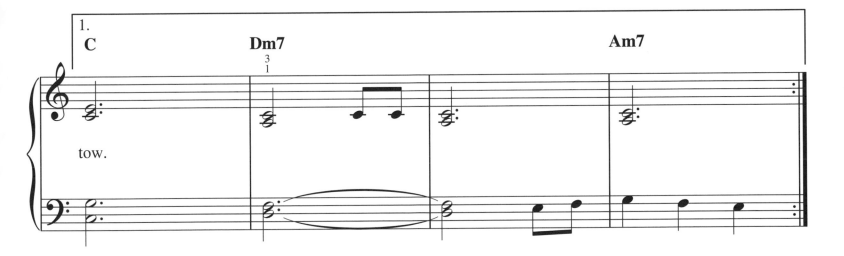

1.
C   **Dm7**   **Am7**

tow.

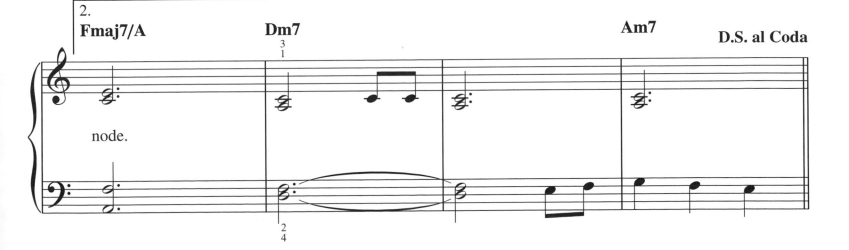

2.
Fmaj7/A   **Dm7**   **Am7**   **D.S. al Coda**

node.

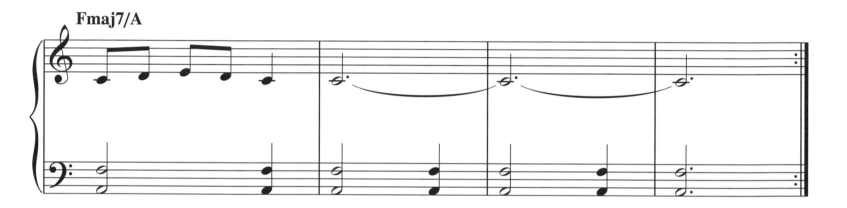

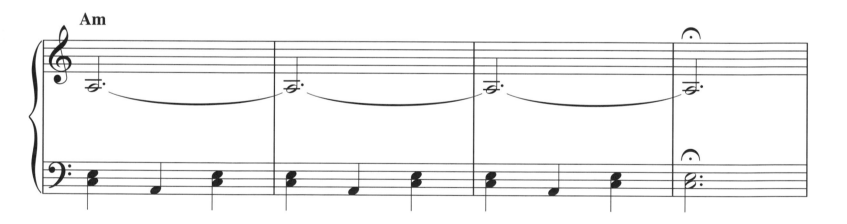

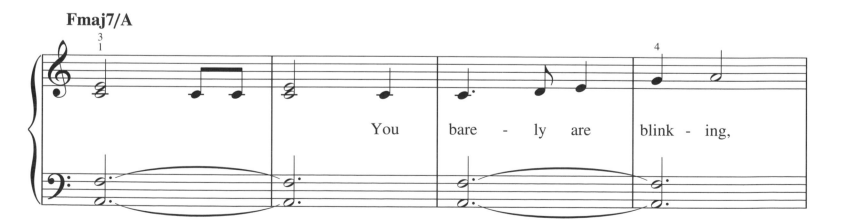

You bare - ly are blink - ing,

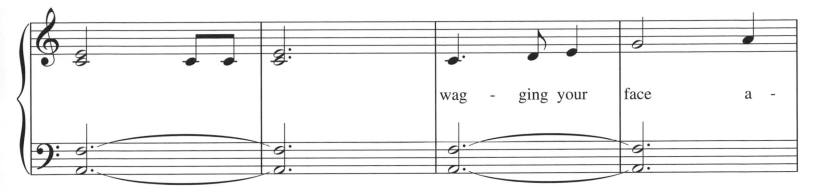

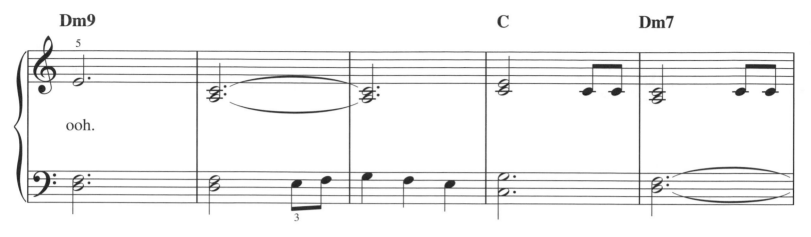

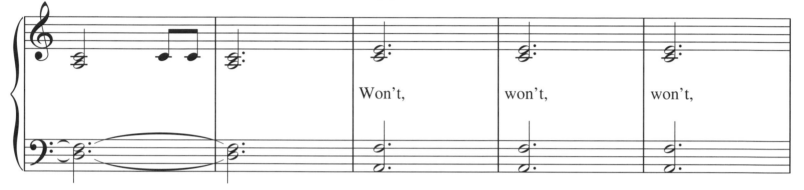

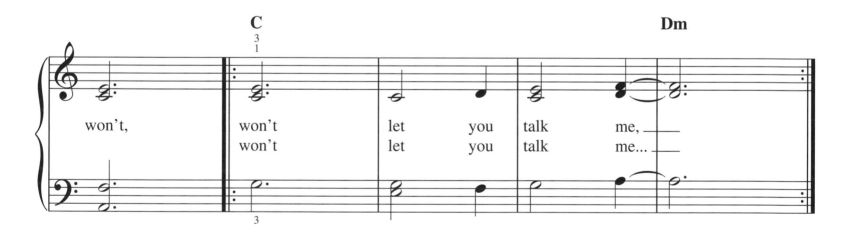

Fmaj7/A

Will pull it

C

taut, noth - ing let

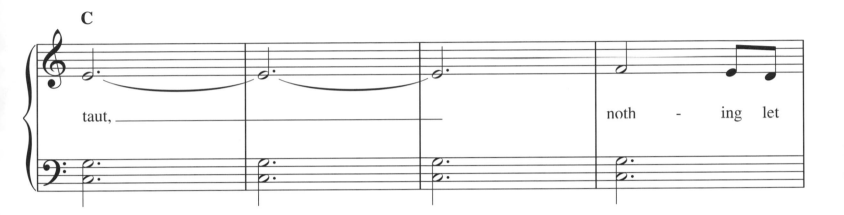

G/D

Slowly
Am

out.

Fmaj7

DONE ALL WRONG

Words and Music by PETER HAYES
and ROBERT BEEN

Moderately, in 2

With pedal

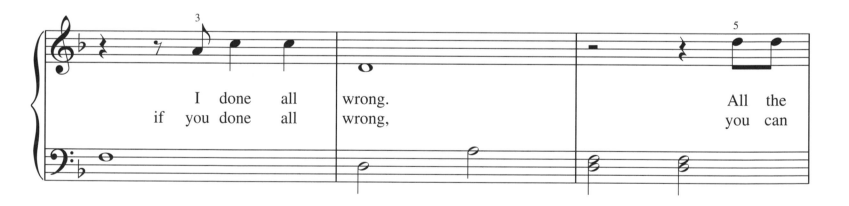

I done me wrong, —
wrong, —

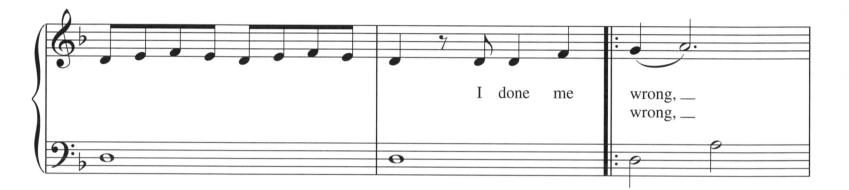

I done all wrong.
if you done all wrong,

All the
you can

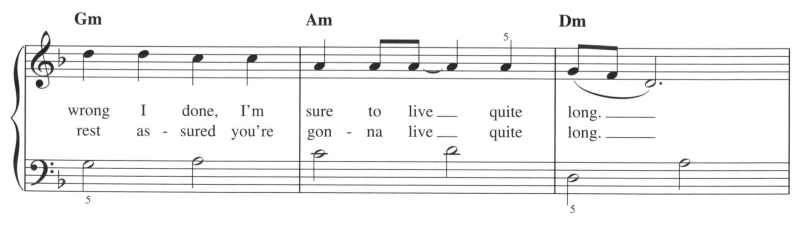

wrong I done, I'm sure to live — quite long. —
rest as-sured you're gon-na live — quite long. —

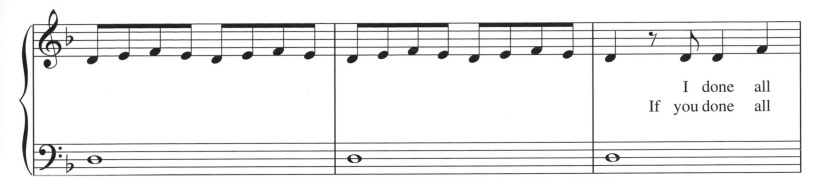

I done all
If you done all

wrong, —
wrong, —

I done me wrong.
you're do - ing wrong,

Gm   **Am**

All the wrong I done, I'm
you can rest as - sured you're

sure to live — quite, —
gon - na live — quite, —

Dm

— quite long. ——
— quite long. ——

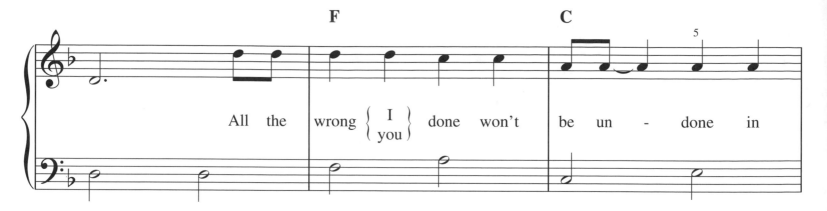

All the wrong ⎰ I ⎱ done won't be un - done in
⎱ you ⎰

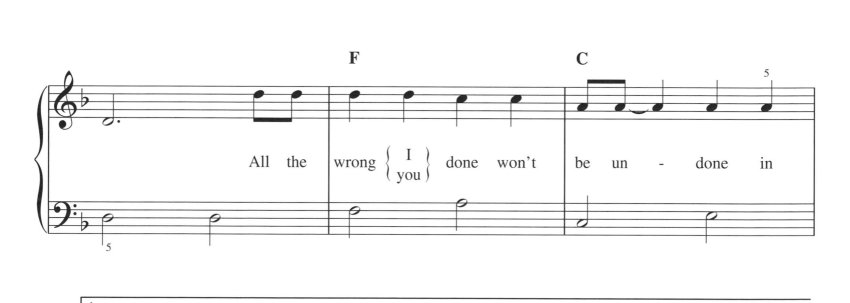

song.

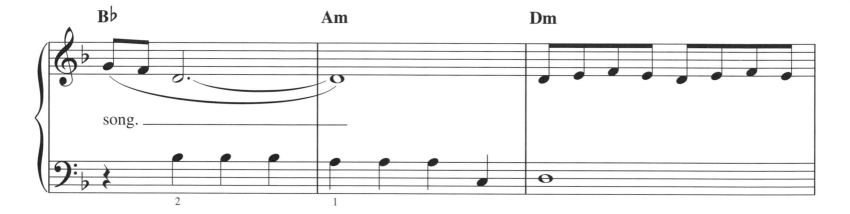

All the wrong ⎰ I ⎱ done won't be un - done in
⎱ you ⎰

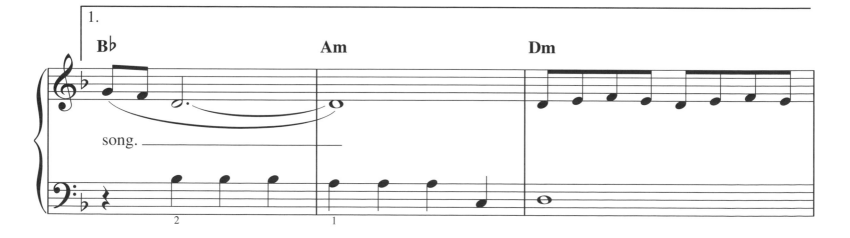

1.

song.

If you're do - ing

song. _____ We're do - ing

wrong, _ we all done _ wrong. If we

done no wrong, I'm sure we would _ be gone. _____

MONSTERS

Words and Music by
STEVE SCHLITZ

Moderately fast

Sit - u - a - tions are crit - i - cal; _____ you
mon - sters are bur - ied down deep in - side. _____ You

got - ta look first be - fore you go. _____ If you
nev - er know when they're sat - is - fied. _____

was - n't too sure, then now you know __
Bur - ied down deep where the sun don't shine, __

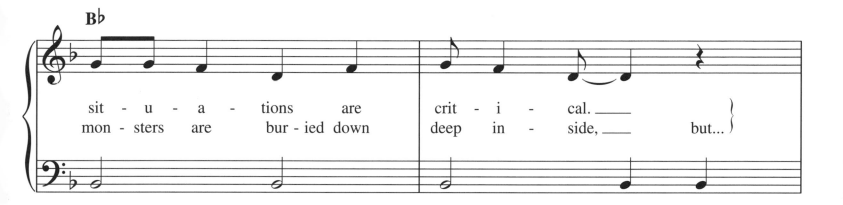

sit - u - a - tions are crit - i - cal. ____
mon - sters are bur - ied down deep in - side, ____ but...

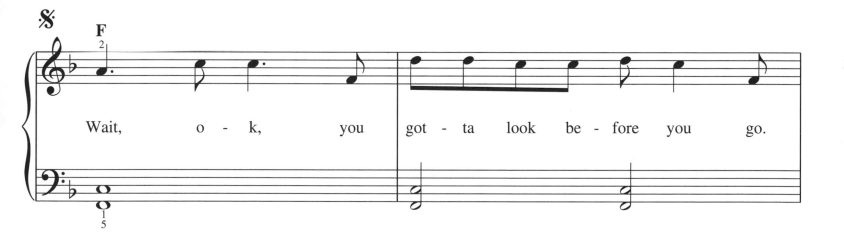

Wait, o - k, you got - ta look be - fore you go.

1.

Wait, o - k, you

58

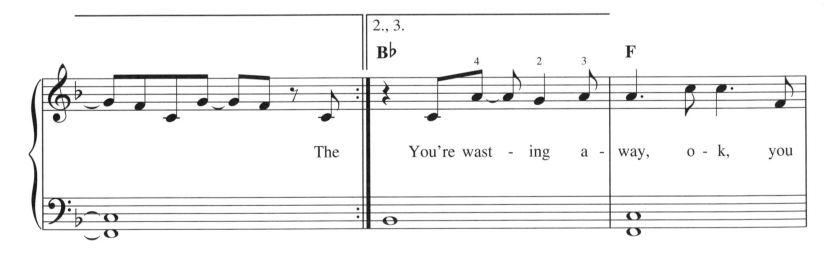

deep in - to the dark - ness where I hide,

deep in - to the dark - ness where I hide.

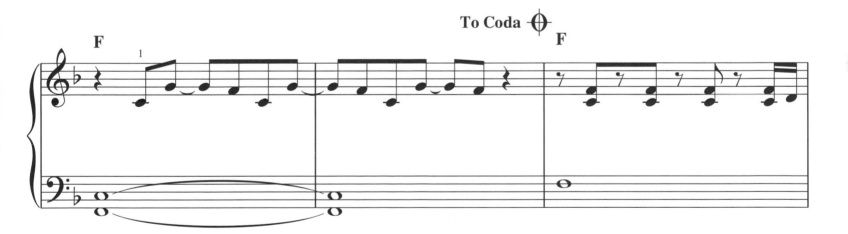

To Coda

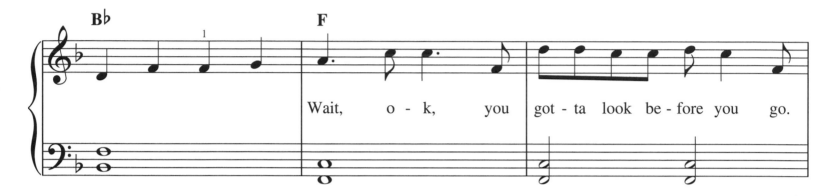

Wait, o - k, you got - ta look be - fore you go.

Deep in - to the

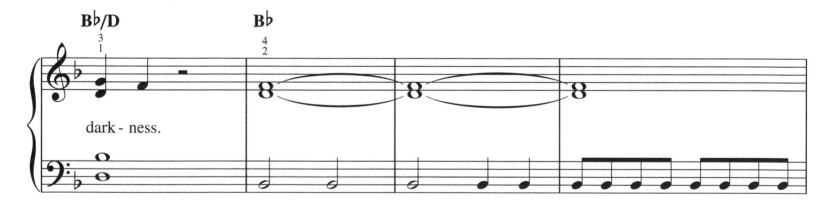

dark - ness.

THE VIOLET HOUR

Words and Music by
ALEX BROWN CHURCH

Moderately fast Pop

Your lips are net - tles, ___
Your arms are love - ly, ___
I turned the lights out. ___

your tongue is wine. ___ Your laugh - ter's
yel - low and rose. ___ Your back's a
I cleaned the sheets. ___ You changed the

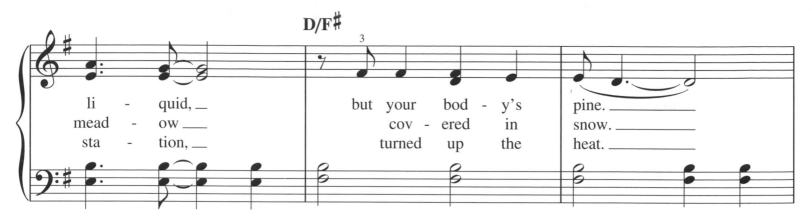

D/F#

li - quid, ___ but your bod - y's pine. ___
mead - ow ___ cov - ered in snow. ___
sta - tion, ___ turned up the heat. ___

G   **Bm/F#**

You love all sail - ors, ___ but hate the
Your thighs are this - tles ___ and hot - house
And now you're sit - ting ___ up - on your

Em

beach. You say, "Come, touch me," ___
grapes. You breathe your sweet breath ___
chair. You've got me tan - gled up

D   **G**

but you're al - ways out ___ of reach.
and have me wait. ___
in - side your beau - ti - ful black hair. In the

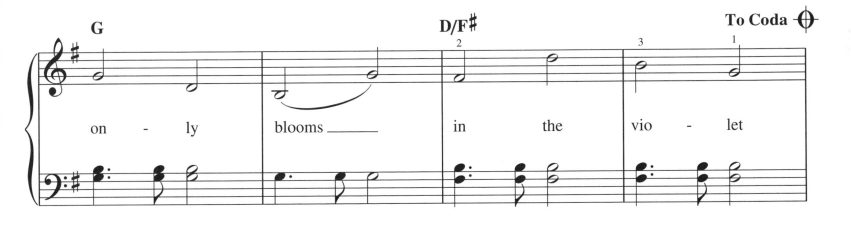

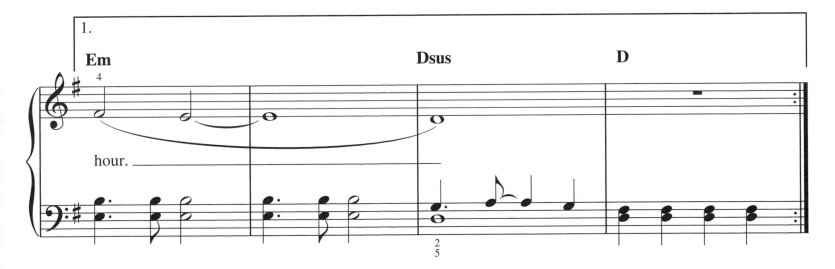

64

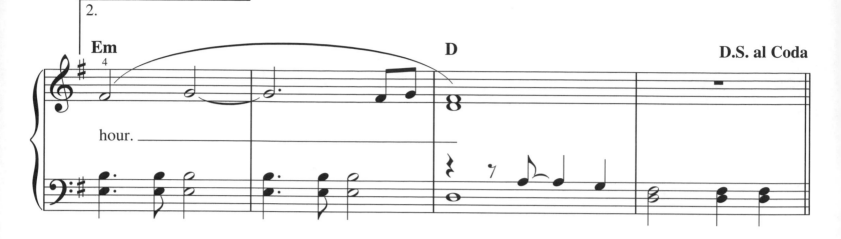

that on - ly

blooms in the vio - let hour.

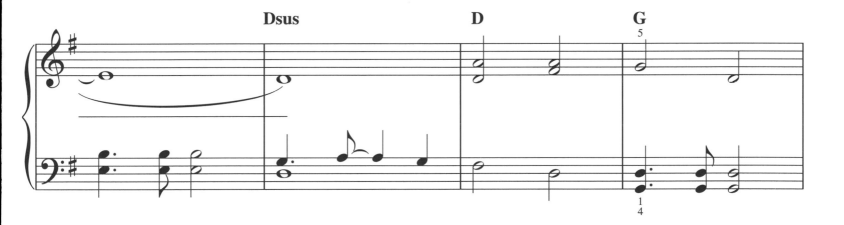

SHOOTING THE MOON

Words and Music by DAMIAN KULASH
and TIM NORDWIND

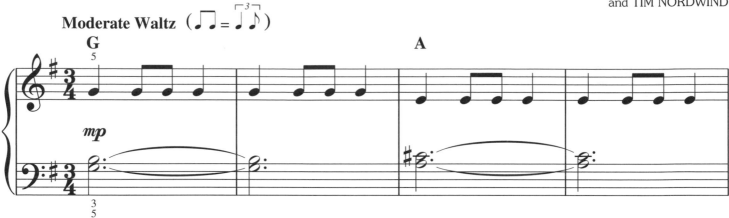

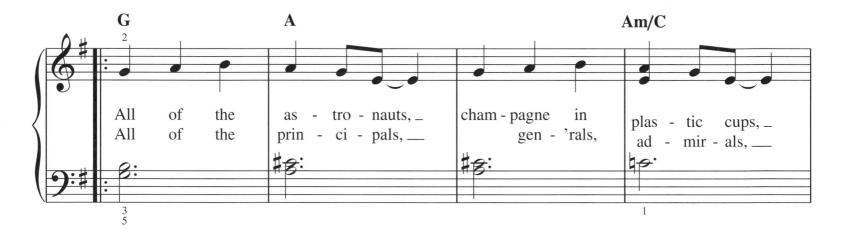

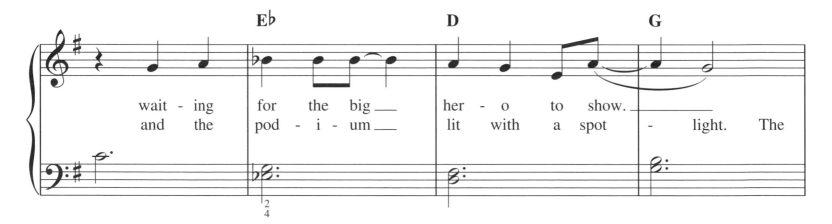

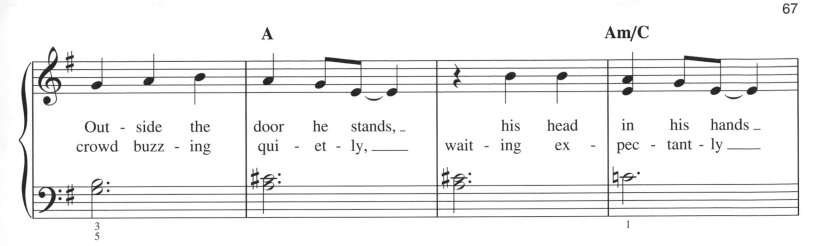

Out - side the door he stands, _ his head in his hands _
crowd buzz - ing qui - et - ly, _____ wait - ing ex - pec - tant - ly _____

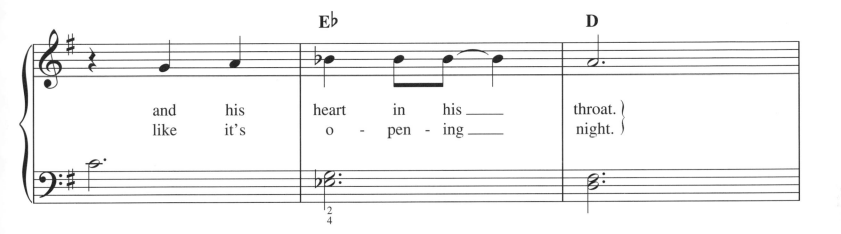

and his heart in his _____ throat. ⎫
like it's o - pen - ing _____ night. ⎭

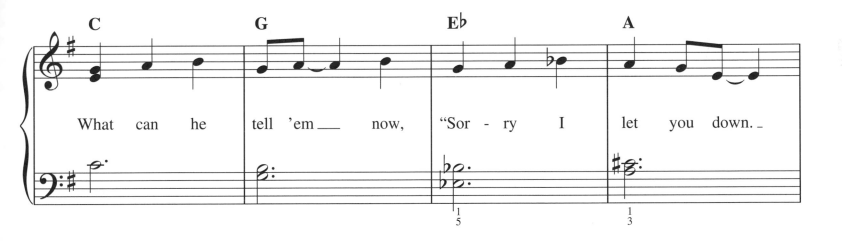

What can he tell 'em _ now, "Sor - ry I let you down. _

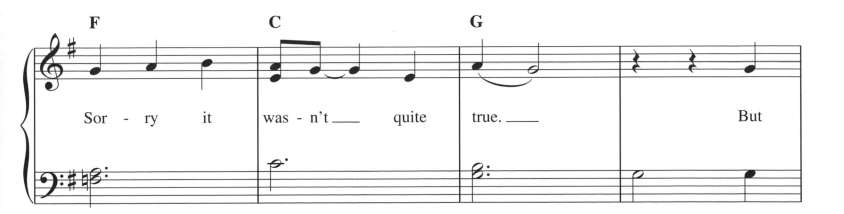

Sor - ry it was - n't _____ quite true. _____ But

don't get hung up on _____ it, just sold - ier

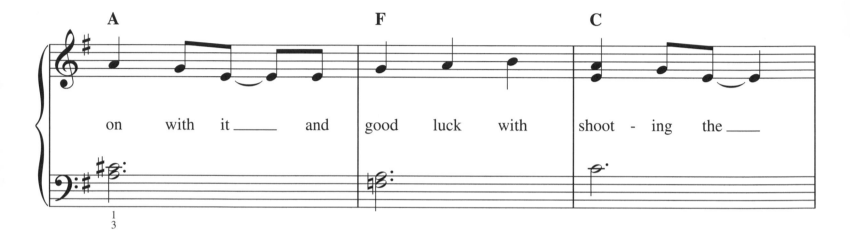

on with it _____ and good luck with shoot - ing the _____

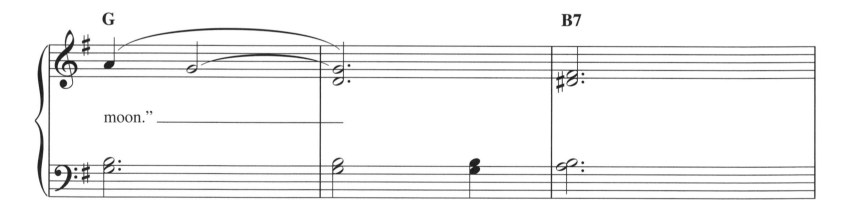

moon." _____

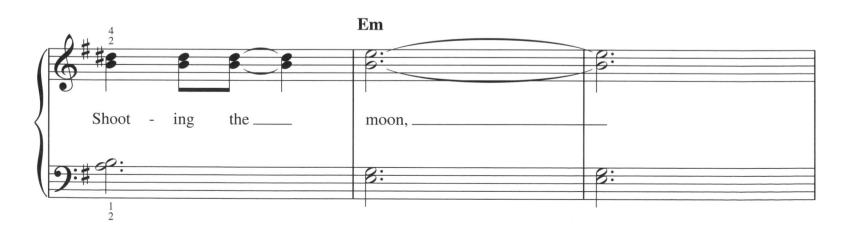

Shoot - ing the _____ moon, _____

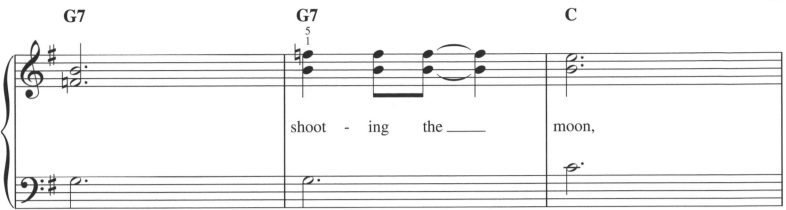

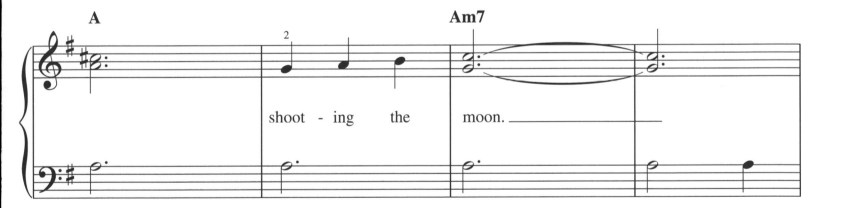

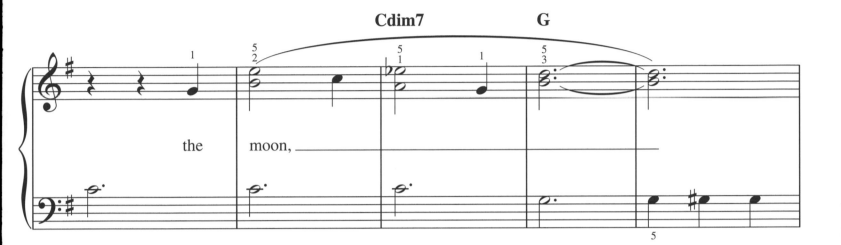

70

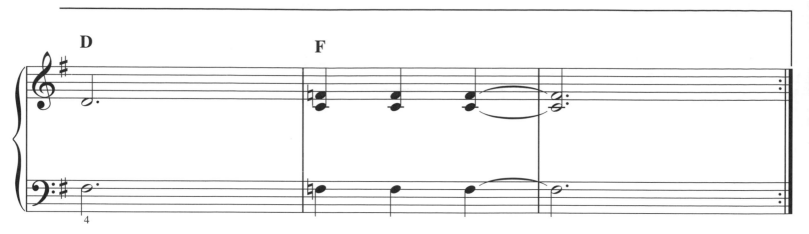

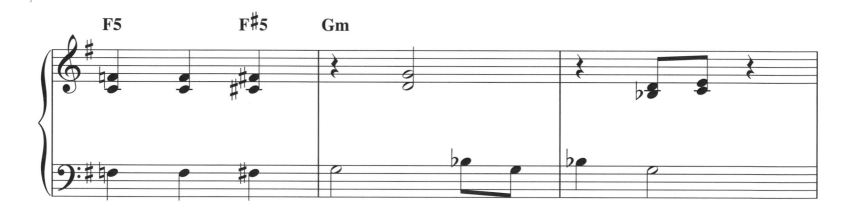

SLOW LIFE

Words and Music by
GRIZZLY BEAR

Slowly, gently

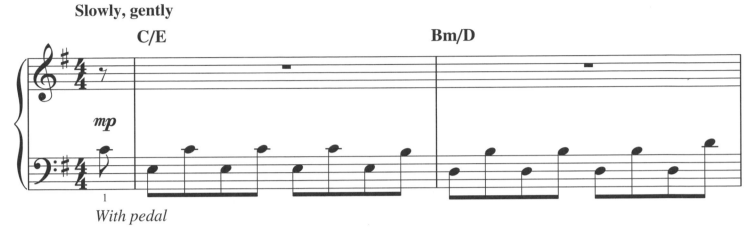

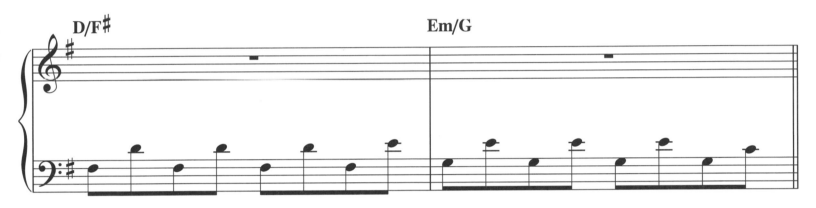

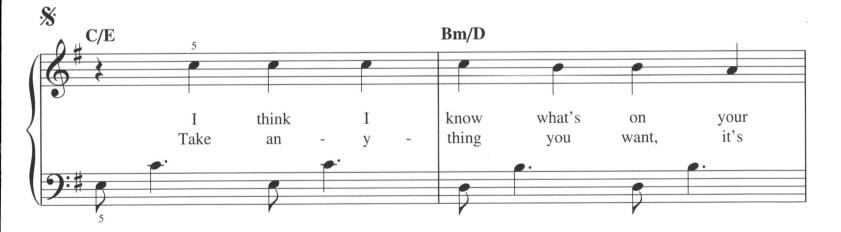

I think I know what's on your mind, _____
Take an - y - thing you want, it's fine. _____

a cou - ple
Keep all the

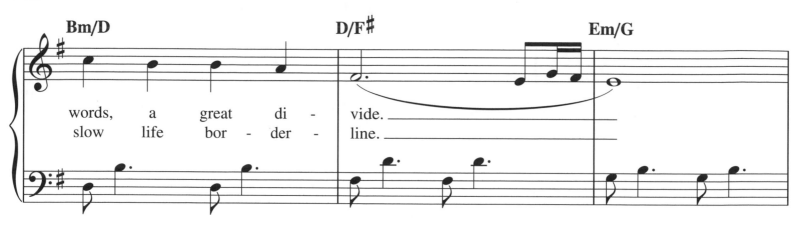

Bm/D ... **D/F#** ... **Em/G**

words, a great di - vide. _____
slow life bor - der - line. _____

C/E ... **Bm/D** ... **D/F#**

Wait - ing in the wings, a small re - spite _____
Don't _ take it back on, just de - ny _____

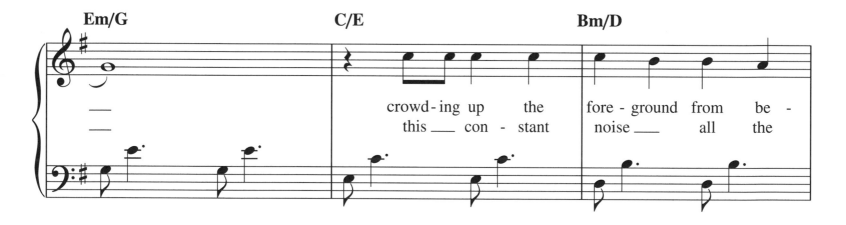

Em/G ... **C/E** ... **Bm/D**

crowd - ing up the fore - ground from be -
this _ con - stant noise _____ all the

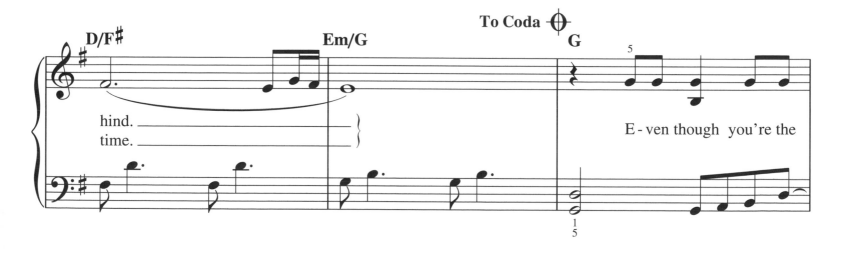

To Coda ⊕

D/F# ... **Em/G** ... **G**

hind. _____
time. _____

E - ven though you're the

5
1
5

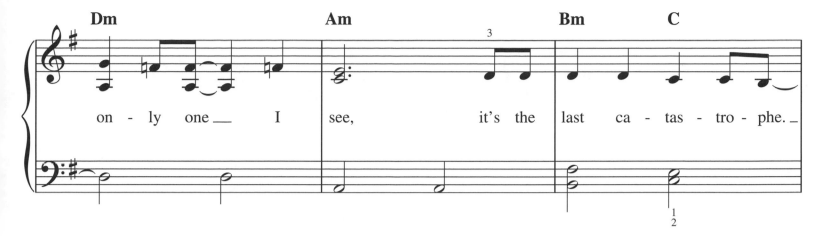

on - ly one __ I see, it's the last ca - tas - tro - phe. __

__ Place your bets on chance and a - pa - thy.

D.S. al Coda

CODA

E-ven though you're the on - ly one __ I

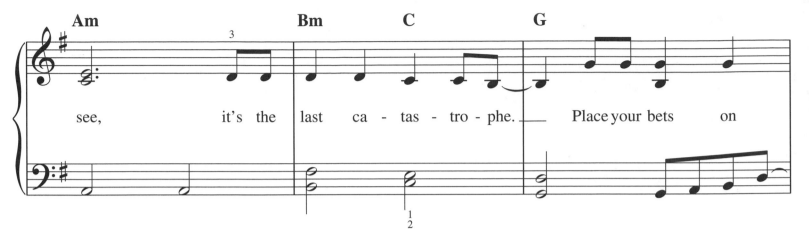

see, it's the last ca - tas - tro - phe. Place your bets on

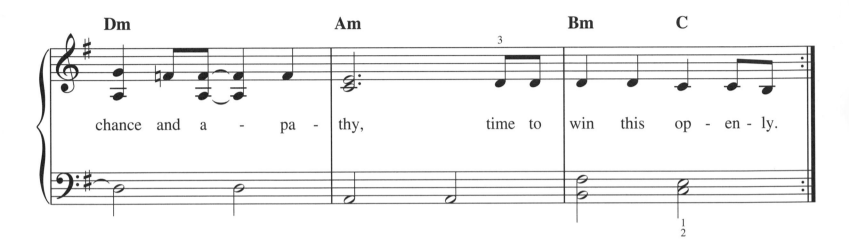

chance and a - pa - thy, time to win this op - en - ly.

E - ven though you're the on - ly one ___ I see.

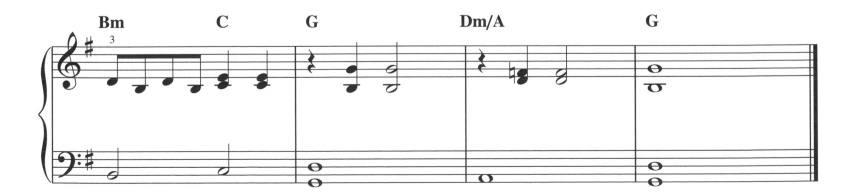

NO SOUND BUT THE WIND

Words and Music by TOM SMITH,
CHRIS URBANOWICZ,
RUSSELL LEETCH and ED LAY

Moderately, with feeling

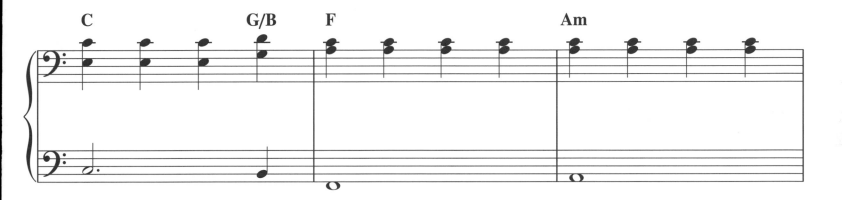

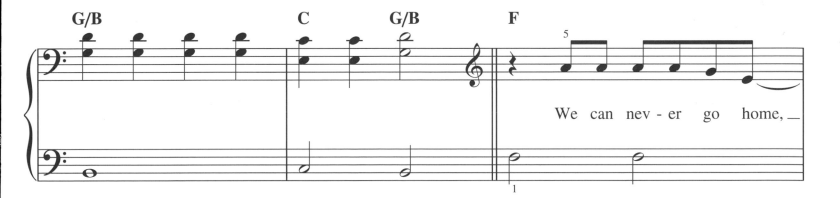

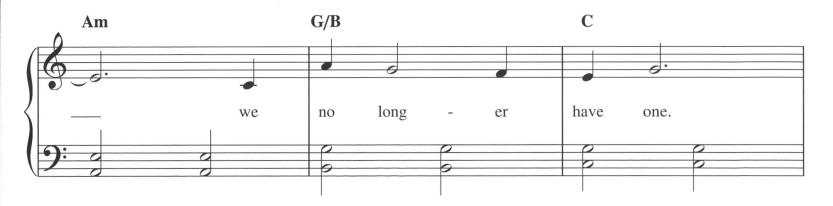

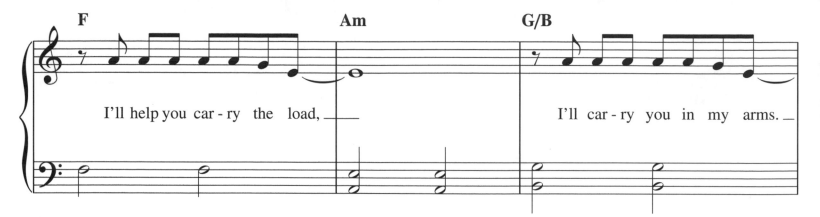

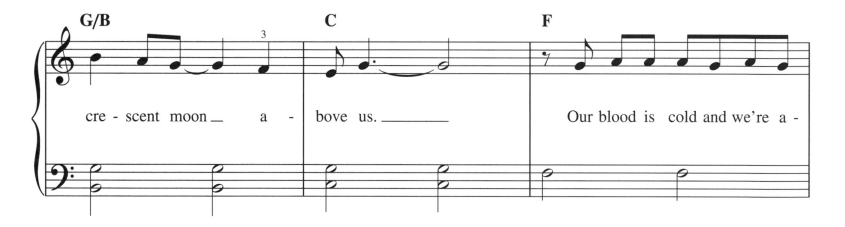

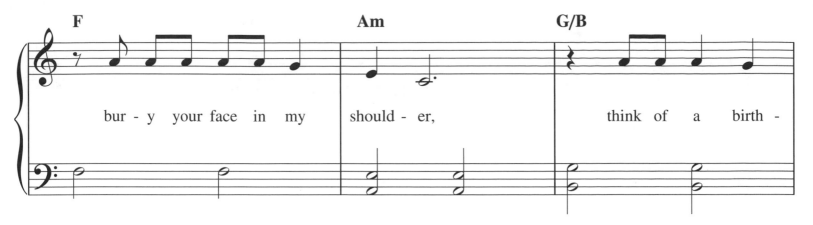

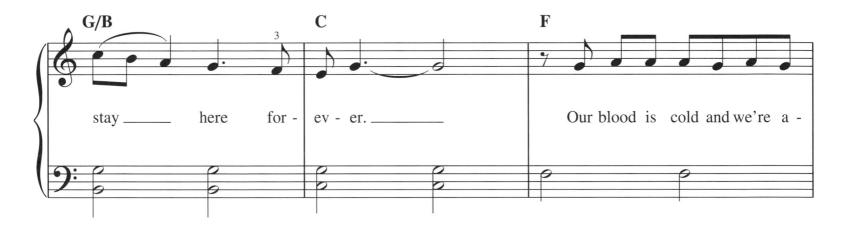

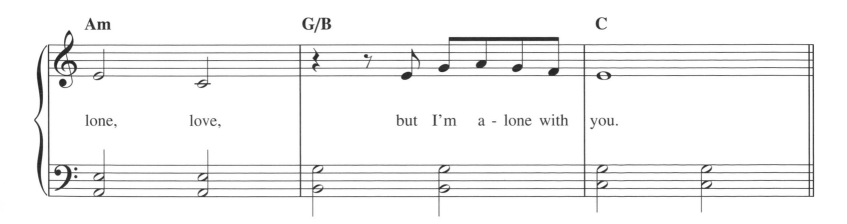

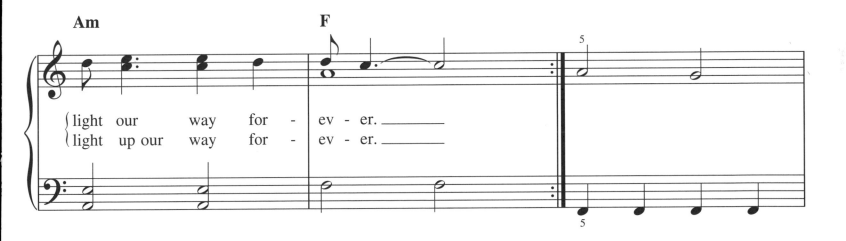

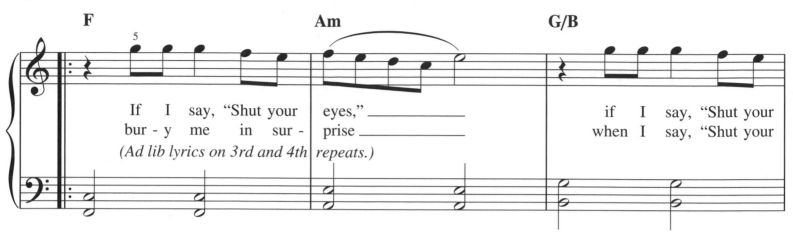

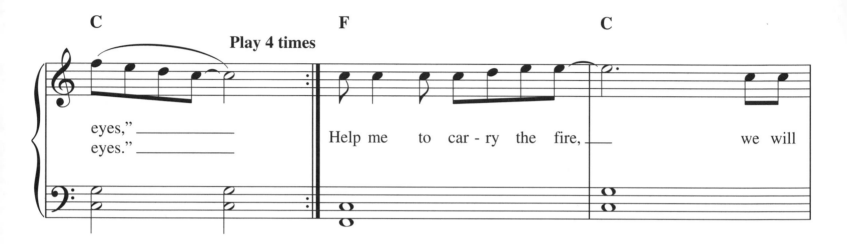

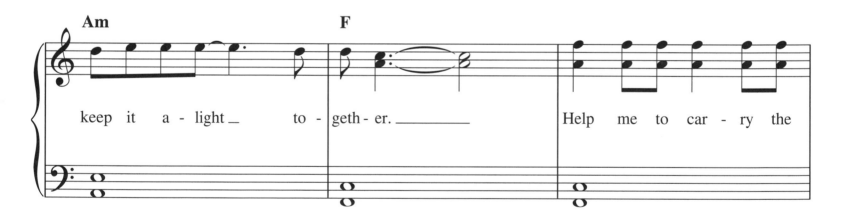

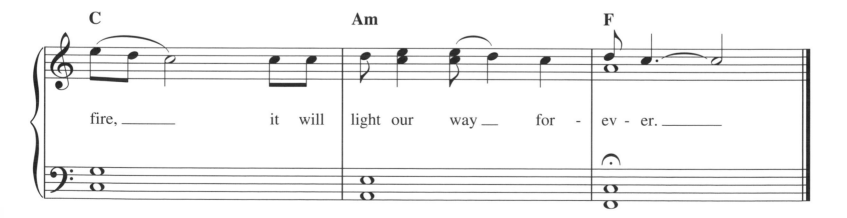

NEW MOON
(The Meadow)

Composed by
ALEXANDRE DESPLAT

Moderately, with feeling

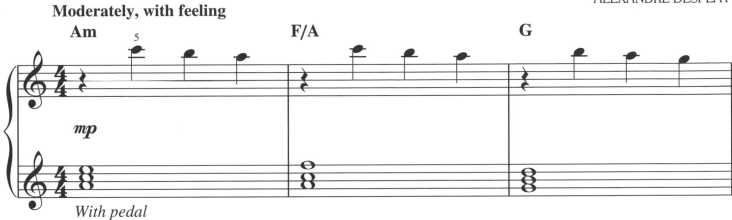

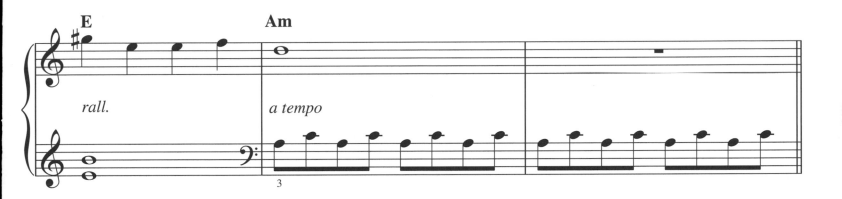

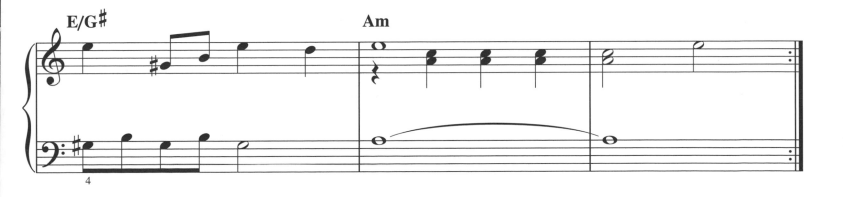

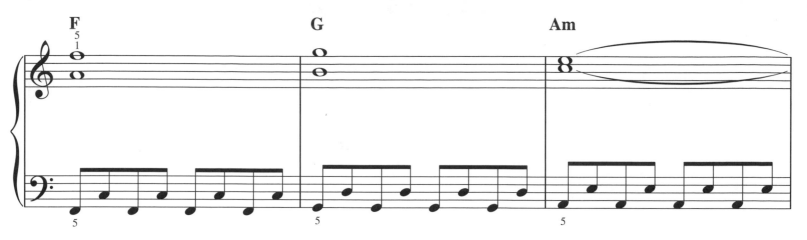

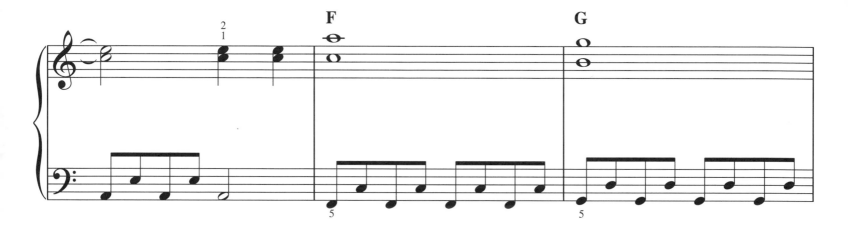

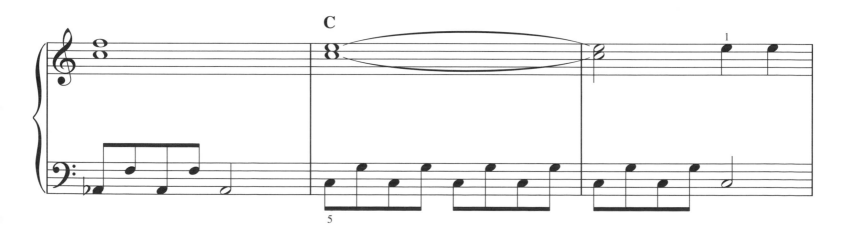

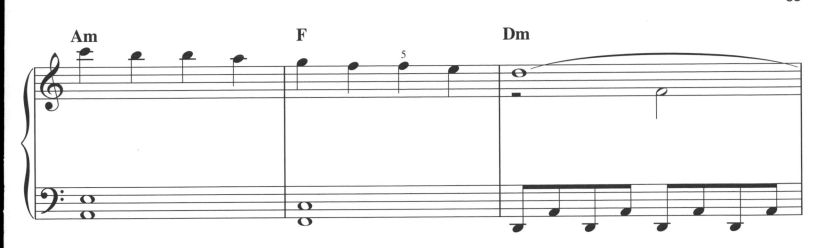

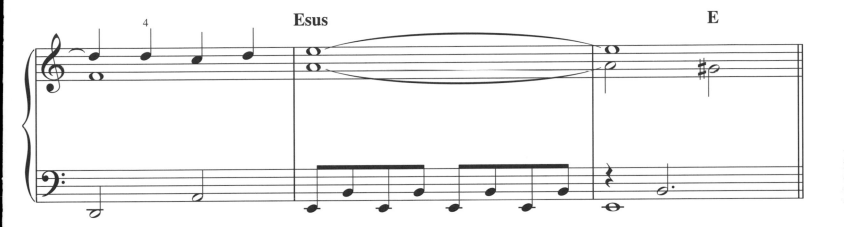

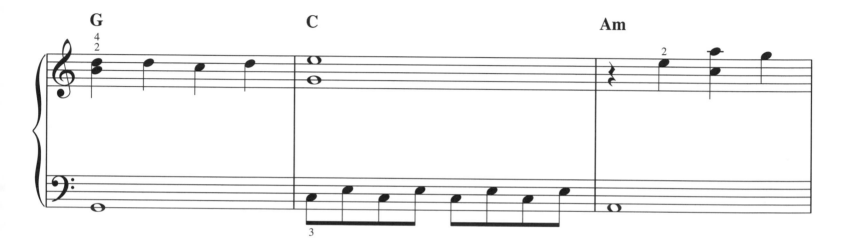

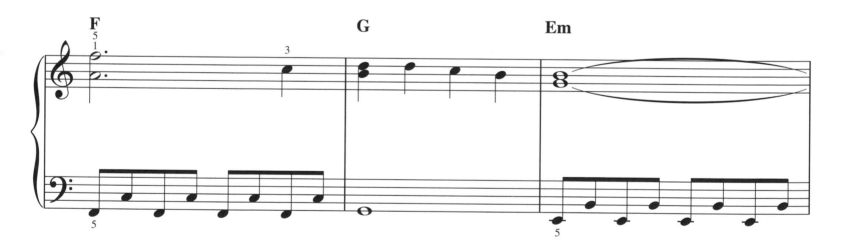

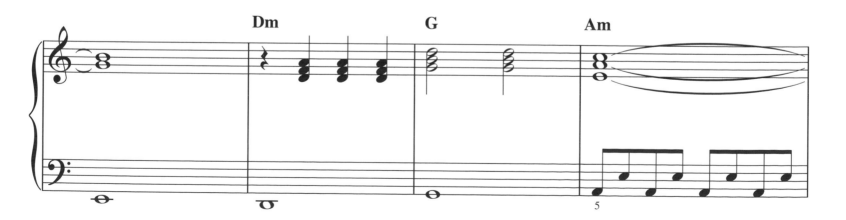

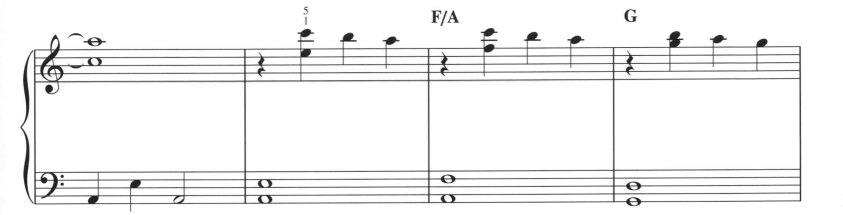

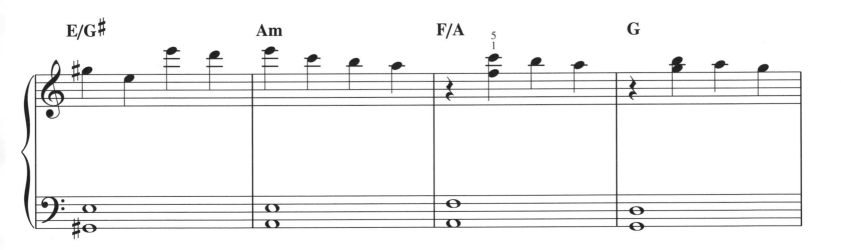

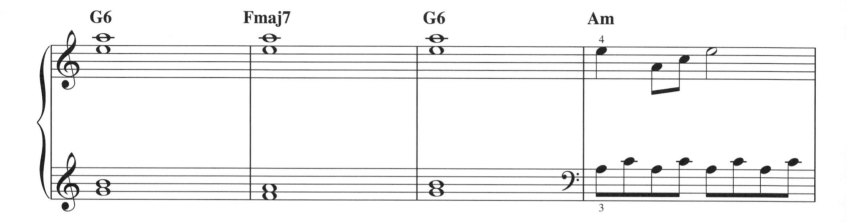

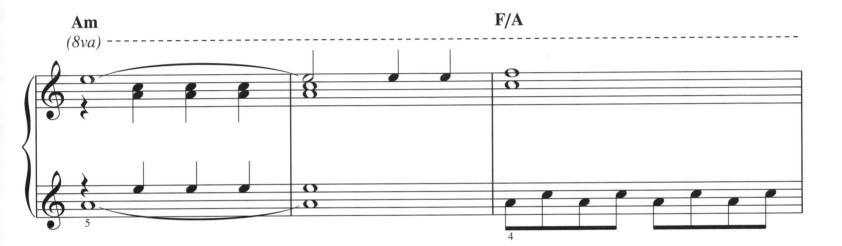

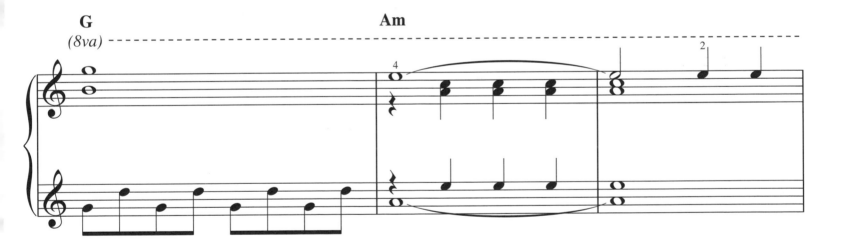

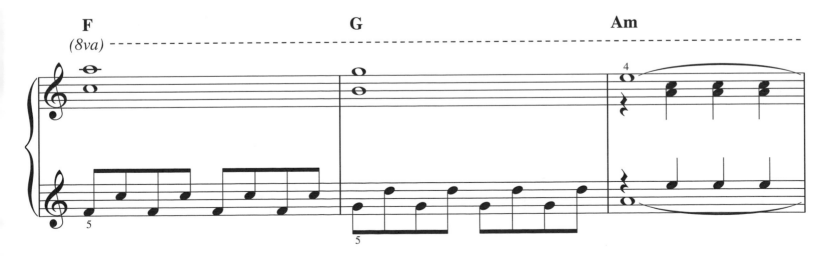

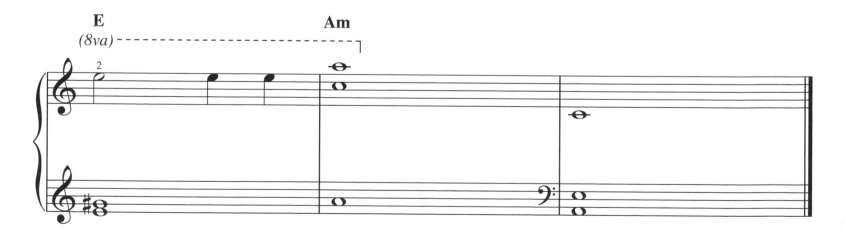